D1084171

LONG ROAD FROM
QUITO

LONG ROAD FROM

QUITO

Transforming Health Care
in Rural Latin America

TONY HISS

University of Notre Dame Press

Notre Dame, Indiana

University of Notre Dame Press
Notre Dame, Indiana 46556
undpress.nd.edu

Published in the United States of America

Library of Congress Cataloging-in-Publication Data

Names: Hiss, Tony, author.
Title: Long road from Quito : transforming health care in rural Latin America
  / Tony Hiss.
Description: Notre Dame, Indiana : University of Notre Dame Press, [2019] |
  Identifiers: LCCN 2018055516 (print) | LCCN 2018059953 (ebook) | ISBN
  9780268105358 (pdf) | ISBN 9780268105365 (epub) | ISBN 9780268105334
  (hardback : alk. paper) | ISBN 0268105332 (hardback : alk. paper)
Subjects: LCSH: Gaus, David. | Physicians—United States—Biography. |
  Physician executives—United States—Biography. | Andean Health and
  Development (Organization) | Medical care—Ecuador. | Medical care—Latin
  America. | Health services accessibility—Ecuador. | Health services
  accessibility—Latin America.
Classification: LCC R154. G218 (ebook) | LCC R154. G218 H57 2019 (print) |
DDC
  610.92 [B] —dc23
LC record available at https://lccn.loc.gov/2018055516

∞*This paper meets the requirements of ANSI/NISO Z39.48-1992*
(Permanence of Paper).

Contents

Map of Ecuador, © *OpenStreetMap contributors*

Foreword

During our senior year at Notre Dame in 1984, I was fortunate to come to know David Gaus. We actually grew rather close as we discerned together our calling to serve the poor in Latin America. David traveled to Quito, Ecuador, while I ventured off to Santiago, Chile. We exchanged letters from time to time over the next couple of years. I recall David lamenting, in one particular missive, that he had experienced repeated bouts of lice while playing with the children at the Centro Muchacho Trabajador, or the Working Boys Center, which assisted the boys and their entire families. The physician counseled David to stop wrestling around with the little children. Instead, David wrote, he opted to shave his head. "I need the warmth and affection as much as, if not more than, the kids," he explained.

As we were nearing completion of our service I wrote David proposing that we start an orphanage together somewhere in Latin America. His response caught me by surprise. He recounted how the terrible health conditions and unnecessary suffering of the Ecuadorian poor had left an indelible mark on his soul. Along the way, he had discovered his calling: to become a medical doctor, with a public health degree, so he could return to Ecuador to pioneer a sustainable health care model for the marginalized and indigent, especially the rural poor, who had little to no access to health care. I could feel his passion and determination jump off the page as I read his scribbled cursive. There were, however, more than a few obstacles to overcome. For one, David had a bachelor's degree in accounting. He would have to return to college as an undergraduate for two years of pre-medicine classes, then get admitted to a medical school with a tropical medicine concentration—and somehow do all this without incurring any debt. That was enough to dissuade most folks from even getting started.

Never underestimate a bold vision combined with fierce determination. The purity of David's call and the depth of his passion were positively contagious. Albert Einstein declared that there are two ways to approach life: one, as if nothing were a miracle, and the other as if everything were a miracle. Spearheaded by David's inspiration, his close friend, Fr. Ted Hesburgh, C.S.C., helped line up a series of miracle workers who repeatedly stepped up to help make David's vision become a reality.

There is much more, however, to David's story than the innovative model and amazing impact of Andean Health and Development. While in medical school, David married an Ecuadorian. Elizabeth, a young woman from a destitute family at the Centro Muchacho Trabajador, joined David at Tulane on a three-month fiancée visa. Elizabeth's journey from bone-crushing poverty to a new world, learning English, and achieving a college degree as an educator, is nothing short of a miracle itself. Together David and Elizabeth brought three beautiful and loving children into this world. And together as a team, Elizabeth and David led the way to high-quality health care for countless rural Ecuadorians who had been excluded from any health care whatsoever.

If you are lucky, a few times in life you will come across a person who is able to hew out of the mountain of despair a stone of hope. It is even rarer still to find in such a leader a genuine sense of humility and a depth of soul that radiates joy and laughter. I know you will enjoy and be inspired by this story of a modern-day man who is as holy as he is innovative, who is as determined as he is fun, and who is both visionary and focused on the set of eyes before him at any given moment.

Lou Nanni

CHAPTER ONE

ROSA

MY FIRST SUSTAINED LOOK AT DAVID GAUS, A SUNNY, energetic, all-American-looking Midwestern doctor in the midst of transforming rural health care in Ecuador, was a wide shot. It was late one night a few years ago, and, having just cleared customs, I was standing with my bag gazing across the vast, bright, gleamingly clean arrivals hall of the then-brand-new Quito airport, past a slowly thinning crowd of groggy travelers. It's one of those twenty-first-century people-processing places—interchangeable, windowless, and of course air-conditioned—where everyone's main purpose seems to be to find the exit as fast as possible, though the room itself may have an add-on purpose, which is to let arriving passengers know that a country that can construct such a room has arrived on the world stage. Blandness is a form of boasting. So is discontinuity. Nowhere are there any reminders of the 1960 airport that used to be: a once out-in-the-cornfields terminal that the city, now seven times larger, engulfed decades ago;

1

its runway was so close to nearby mountainsides that right away it became notorious for steeply-angled "white-knuckle" takeoffs and landings.

The new, too-big arrivals hall, an area where life is on temporary hold until it's clear that rules have been followed, was designed on another continent by Canadian architects and deliberately not built for drama. In this case one was taking place anyway. In a far corner, Gaus, six-foot-one and still boyish in his early fifties, with long eyelashes that embarrassed him as a kid, had a large, rectangular black box at his feet and was engaged in a courteous but intense and extended conversation with two uniformed customs officers. The anonymous box, which Gaus had just opened, could've contained just about anything, but to my mind had a look of super-reinforced seriousness that suggested the kind of plain-looking, oversized, fortified-at-the-edges case that golf pros or top-of-the-line musicians buy when they have to fly with something awkwardly shaped, easily damaged, and worth thousands or even tens of thousands of dollars. Maybe a contra bass trombone, which, though made of solid metal, is widely considered exceptionally fragile.

But it wasn't a trombone Gaus was matter-of-factly and without fanfare seeking to bring into the country along with rest of his (drama-free) checked luggage. The puzzled-looking customs men were staring dubiously at a full-sized, remarkably lifelike, high-fidelity plastic mannequin of a woman with light skin and dark hair. Her mouth slightly agape, she was, as I could see even from across the room, sightlessly gazing upward through ever-open eyes, a stillness surrounded by a swirling throng.

This striking apparition was a SimMom, a high-tech ob/gyn teaching mannequin or, as its manufacturer calls it, an "advanced full-body birthing simulator," which, when operational, can seem to breathe and bleed and which comes complete with a SimNewB, a sim (simulated) newborn still attached to a pizza-shaped placenta. SimMoms—products, like the airport, of another continent—come provided with *norteamericano* names like Noelle and Victoria, but Gaus had already named this one Rosa.

SimMoms have become a somewhat familiar sight among doctors in the United States, where, since the 1990s, more than three hundred medical schools and teaching hospitals have set up simulation centers as part of a new way of training doctors and nurses. So far, though, there are only three such facilities in Ecuador—a tiny one in the country's biggest city and commercial capital, the historic southerly port of Guayaquil, on the Pacific Ocean; a larger one in Quito, the nine-thousand-feet-plus-high capital city in the north, which was founded almost two thousand years ago, long before the Incas; and the one where Rosa was heading, a sim center that Gaus and a small nonprofit group of Ecuadorian doctors had opened three months earlier in Santo Domingo de los Colorados, a city in the middle of the ranches and banana plantations of the Northwestern countryside that's suddenly the third-largest, and in many ways most fascinating, city in Ecuador, although still tourist-shunned and yet-to-be-beautiful. A half century ago, this city that emerged almost overnight was a small, dusty village with a couple of unpaved streets way off in the heart of what was still mile after mile of virgin forest. Often called Santo for short, Santo Domingo is just as often referred to as the rural capital of Ecuador.

Rosa, finally, was on her way to Santo, once Gaus had concluded his prolonged talk with the customs people. This highly complex $30,000 machine, a sophisticated piece of modern medical technology, had been cleared for entry into Ecuador, with smiles and handshakes all around. Rosa could now become an everyday teaching tool in a tropical community in the western foothills of the Andes that the cosmopolitan residents of Quito, *los quiteños*, only about eighty miles upslope, consider remote and think of primarily as a place to navigate through on a day-long drive down to the Pacific Ocean beaches.

I got to witness this particular transaction, Rosa's unorthodox, late-night appearance in the country, most likely unnoticed by the other bleary-eyed travelers, because I'd heard about David Gaus through friends and become intrigued. So I'd gone to Ecuador to meet him and observe his work firsthand. It's highly unusual, though not unheard-of, for U.S. physicians to spend much of their lives in the developing world. The most celebrated of these doctors is Paul Farmer, winner of a MacArthur Foundation Genius Grant, who in his twenties opened a one-room clinic in a destitute town in the Haitian countryside. Partners in Health, the organization Farmer founded, now has facilities and programs in ten countries and is constructing a University of Global Health Equity on a 250-acre campus in Rwanda. In 2001 Scott Kellermann, chief of staff at a California hospital, sold his home and moved to Uganda for eight years to work with the impoverished Batwa pygmies, who had a life expectancy of twenty-eight years; they'd been evicted from the Bwindi Impenetrable Forest, their ancestral homeland, when it got turned into a national park to protect endangered mountain gorillas. Kellermann's open-air clinic under a ficus tree has given way to a 112-bed hospital, one of the best in Uganda. He and his wife, Carol, an educator, have built homes, started schools, and set up a foundation. In 2014 both Kellermanns were honored by the Dalai Lama as Unsung Heroes of Compassion.

Other non-M.D.s from the United States have also helped cure people far from home. In 1973 David Werner, a high-school biology teacher who'd been living in mountain villages in western Mexico with no electricity and connected only by mule trails, wrote *Donde no hay doctor* (Where There Is No Doctor), a health guide for the most isolated of communities; since then it has been translated into one hundred languages, with three million copies now in print. I'd known about these extraordinary people when I heard about Gaus—there was something compelling, friends told me, about the way Gaus and his Ecuadorian colleagues were promoting widespread and radical changes in rural health care with a series of partly imported, partly on-the-spot, and very often under-the-radar and altogether unexpected methods. Now that I'd seen Gaus in action, talking Rosa through customs, I was ready to see more.

Since that night I've come to know Gaus and his family— his wife is Ecuadorian and his three bilingual children have dual American and Ecuadorian citizenship—and many of his colleagues at Andean Health and Development (AHD), the nonprofit he co-founded in 1996 with his first mentor, Fr. Theodore Hesburgh—"Fr. Ted" to his legions of admirers, who by then was president emeritus of the University of Notre Dame in South Bend, Indiana. His later mentors, Gaus says, have been the people of Ecuador and the doctors who are his partners: One of them grew up in a tiny town in the Ecuadorian Amazon region far below the eastern slope of the Andes; another, his closest associate, is the grand-nephew of a former president and grew up scampering through the rooms of the Ecuadorian White House.

I've had the chance to visit and explore both of his rural outposts—the two hospitals AHD has built since the turn of the century, the newer one in Santo, with sixty beds (the sim center is part of it), and the one that opened in 2001, with seventeen beds, in a farming town some fifty miles to the north that's as unhistoric as Santo, being about the same age but staying the same size that Santo was fifty years ago. This second town, a place quiet enough and so informal that you can hear roosters crowing outside during early-morning staff conferences, is sort of dwarfed by its grandly rolling name, Pedro Vicente Maldonado, a tribute to the first Ecuadorian scientist to achieve an international reputation, back in the eighteenth century. The country's only Antarctic research base is also named after Maldonado, an astronomer who created the first meticulously detailed map of Ecuador, later spent seven years building a road through the rainforest from Quito to the coast, and died young; the road barely survived him. The town that bears his name is called Pedro, for short. Hospital Pedro Vicente Maldonado serves the people of Pedro and the surrounding three-county countryside—five thousand in the town and seventy thousand altogether. Previously, none had had access to a hospital. The doors of the two AHD hospitals, in Pedro and Santo are open to all, whether they can afford to pay or not—this is a bedrock principle. And both hospitals have been finding ways to pay for themselves, another foundational principle.

I've been impressed by Gaus's good humor, patience, and energy, as well as by the way he can immediately take people seriously and befriend almost anyone, whether they're patients or ambassadors or airport officials; it's a kind of innate bedside manner. To work effectively in the countryside, Gaus has very much become a tri-cultural person. He's fluent in a self-taught Spanish he calls a "unique gringo thing," which somehow combines a Wisconsin twang with a bit of a musical Quito overlay (*quiteños* tend to add p's and f's to words ending in vowels, so the name of the city becomes Quitop or Quitoff). He's also someone who understands the customs and even the unspoken thoughts of rural folk that are altogether opaque to many of the urbanite graduates from Ecuador's top medical schools who come to the AHD hospitals as young physicians and residents.

In getting close to Gaus and his work over several years, I've been captivated perhaps most by a quality I'd never quite encountered before—his continuing, unswerving, indeed constantly escalating ability to jump at new possibilities, a capacity that has led him to meet setbacks that come his way with energy and flexibility and even a dash of inspiration so as to expand, amend, outgrow, and enrich his vision of how many people he and his staff can help and the nature of the gift they can then offer Ecuador, a country Gaus first went to somewhat by chance in 1984.

That was the summer after his graduation from Notre Dame, when, he said, he had a midlife crisis at the age of 21. It began as a strong feeling that, even though the accounting degree he'd just earned had already produced some well-paying job offers, maybe his life could have more meaning if he didn't become an accountant like his father and grandfather—something which, growing up in Milwaukee, he'd always assumed was exactly what he wanted and would undoubtedly lead to a big home with a view of Lake Michigan in the maple-studded Milwaukee neighborhood of Shorewood, about eight miles east of his own more middle-class neighborhood on the west side of the city. He'd also had real talent as a baseball player, a leftie outfielder and power hitter, but had given that up at Notre Dame when he broke his thumb one week into the fall season. It turned out that a volunteer position was available at a Catholic charity in Quito that helped shoeshine boys and their families. So he filled that position, and overnight his life, which otherwise over decades might have pulled him no farther away from home than several ZIP codes, shifted three thousand miles due south.

Two years after graduation, still in Quito, Gaus realized that if he worked harder than he ever had, maybe he could help some, even if only a few, of the Ecuadorians he'd been getting to know and admire, people who to North American eyes looked ordinary enough in jeans and T-shirts but who, despite this, he had been shocked to find, seldom if ever saw a doctor from the day they were born until they day they died. Gaus decided he could become a doctor back in the States and then return with new skills to a country he felt had given his life purpose. This was the work that over the next eleven years he set out for himself, and, as he was thorough, meant not just getting an M. D. but completing specialized postgraduate training in family medicine and public health and tropical medicine.

Now, after more than twenty years, mostly back in Ecuador, spent doctoring, raising a family, assembling a team, building two hospitals, and setting up programs to train new generations of family physicians for some of the poorest people in Latin America, Gaus is finding a *new* new job. He and his group have reached a point where, if they keep going for a decade or two more, there's a chance they could help Ecuador change the world, or at any rate South America. It has to do with the way people think about their relationship to health and what it is that health brings to families and communities.

One of the things about hanging out with David Gaus is that there are moments you unexpectedly have to scramble to keep up with him, then afterward need to sit a while and think further about. The idea of creating health in Ecuador, for instance, has different underpinnings than you might think, and they become apparent only in retrospect. Common words in an ordinary conversation, I found, resonated in ways I wasn't used to.

Take the word "health" itself. Standard dictionaries cling to what I would now call a half-definition of health, calling it the degree to which a body is free from illness or injury. This presents an odd and anomalous situation, since years back the world officially committed itself to a far more comprehensive definition.

As used by Gaus and here in this book, "health"—sometimes also called "Positive Health"—adheres to the formally established, globally approved meaning first publicly spelled out more than seventy years ago by a much-loved, flamboyant, compelling Croatian physician, Andrija Štampar. Štampar is one of the towering scene-stealers and pioneers who loom behind the twenty-first-century work Gaus and his colleagues are doing. Before World War II, Štampar, in his thirties, set up hundreds of "health stations" and "homes of health" all over Yugoslovia, training villagers to become "the health conscience" of their towns. Then, still in his thirties, he was forced to retire, fired by the king when he refused to become minister of the interior, and soon found himself touring the world as a health advisor for the League of Nations. There is a statue of him in Morocco honoring his work on malaria, while a post-war Yugoslav postage stamp honoring him shows a picture of a scowling round-faced man with owlish glasses. After long stints in China and Latin America, he returned to Yugoslavia shortly before World War II broke out, and within a year he was interned by the Germans.

Just after the war Štampar, at that point called the "Bear of the Balkans," was revered as a figurative giant in twentieth-century public health—at six foot five and massively built, he also literally towered over most of his colleagues. He became a principal author and architect of the constitution of the new United Nations' even newer World Health Organization. He is remembered especially for drafting its preamble, which has since been hailed as the "Magna Carta of health." Its first principle, as adopted by 61 nations in 1946, states explicitly and unequivocally: "Health is a state of complete physical, mental and social well-being and not merely the absence of disease or infirmity." The second principle proclaims health to be "one of the fundamental rights of every human being." Three decades later, in 1978, this definition became a global aspiration when representatives from 134 countries, meeting in Kazakhstan, committed to achieving "Health for All by the Year 2000."

Health, that is, is a "more so" state in which the focus broadens beyond the horizon to include building up strength within and among people in addition to curing and preventing problems. It is positive rather than neutral, something other than a change in emphasis from a glass-half-empty to a glass-half-full perspective, since it has the potential to become cup-runneth-over. Seen this way, the underlying qualities of health remain in existence as long as life lasts, even while diseases come and go—"somewhat like the sky that remains in place," as a recent commentator has suggested, whether or not clouds and storms are present. So establishing health throughout Ecuador—Health for All—would be a singular national accomplishment, a coming of age and an emergence onto the international stage comparable to, and in many ways more ambitious than, a $700 million airport, even one twelve times the size of its predecessor.

Fish, as the novelist David Foster Wallace and others have pointed out, can't see water because they're surrounded by it. In a similar way, it's hard for twenty-first-century North Americans to see their own health—it took a trip to Ecuador for me to get a better glimpse. This health that surrounds us, or many of us (frustratingly and tragically, not all), has a momentum and carries us along like a current—we expect diseases, some serious, to come and go. But by and large an illness, even when it's present, can be considered a temporary interruption, a pause, a sputtering and sidelining—more than a nuisance often enough, but for the most part looked back on in a telescoped way, the pain and discomfort long gone, something successfully surmounted rather than a turning point or the beginning of a downward spiral.

Health is something else again—a presence, as Dr. Štampar suggested, not an absence. Gaus explained the distinction he makes between health and its opposite—for which, he said, John Ruskin had used the word "illth." As an anology, Gaus quoted some famous definitions of peace and its opposite: Martin Luther King Jr. said: "True peace is not merely the absence of tension, it is the presence of justice." Einstein said peace was "the presence of justice, of law, or order—in short, of government." Centuries earlier, the Dutch philosopher Spinoza called peace "a state of mind, a disposition for benevolence, confidence, justice."

Similarly, Gaus suggested, health is a foundation of possibilities. This was striking, because so often medical issues are cast into military terms—the front line in the fight against malaria, the war on cancer. Gaus has taken pains to frame himself and his team in civilian terms, where they're not warriors so much as "health accelerators" whose focus is beyond the battlefield.

Health can be distinguished from "wellness," a popular term in the United States in recent decades, which generally has to do with already being healthy and taking steps to stay that way. Health, in its expanded sense, reaches down to the usually unvoiced level of assumptions people make about how they can enjoyably look forward to retirement and grandchildren. No guarantees, of course, but a likelihood.

And it doesn't depend on conjuring up a never-before utopian vision of the end to all diseases or threats to life and limb. It's more like a damping down of dangers, a shift in emphasis, a realignment of expectations, a lengthening of the odds against something suddenly going very wrong, an ease of mind—*ease* as the opposite of *disease*. In a landscape of health, health can be managed, it can be enhanced, it can be quickly supported, and there will always be someone to turn to at a price that can be afforded. Health doesn't need to be pursued, like happiness. It already is.

If rural Ecuador were to become such a landscape, it would be a profound transformation for its population and a gateway moment for humanity. Displaying this on a map, while of course overgeneralizing somewhat, the 1.2 billion people who live in the developed world have come to think of health as something they and their children can count on (although, as we've said, too many are still left out). That's maybe 15 percent of the global population. The 5.9 billion in the rest of the world, the developing world, have remained in a far more precarious position. Let's color the developed countries green—the United States, Canada, most of Europe, Australia, New Zealand, and maybe a few others, so far all confined to three of the world's continents—and the rest of the world various shades of gray, some lighter, some darker, depending on circumstances.

This is the situation that has remained essentially unchanged for most of a century, despite dramatic advances in treating specific diseases—for instance, hundreds of thousands of people came down with polio in 1990; in 2015, fewer than one hundred people did. What if, over the next decade or two, you could turn one of the lighter gray countries, even a small one like Ecuador, which is only slightly larger than Colorado, green? It wouldn't shift the world's numerical balance. The 16 million Ecuadorians are less than two-tenths of 1 percent of the total population. But it would show that things can change within our lifetime and would stand as the partial fulfillment of the sweeping global goal from Kazakhstan in 1978 of "Health for All by the Year 2000." For the first time since then, a country in the developing world, a country that's also part of a fourth continent, would gain equal standing with wealthier nations in a key area. I suspect that things would move more quickly after that, as this same healthful process could take hold and be adopted in other Andean and South American countries, and in the years that follow updated maps could show parts of still more continents changing color and themselves becoming havens of health.

Gaus himself looks ahead more cautiously, which I found is typical of his assessment of things and might be an attitude that gets ingrained when your life changes not once but again and again, and when you constantly have to leapfrog over wrenching setbacks and challenges. Any one of the interim accomplishments of Gaus and his partners—building a first and then a second rural hospital, founding an unprecedented graduate training program for doctors in rural areas—could be called a happy ending. But that would be the case if they'd been looking for stopping-points instead of stepping-stones.

Gaus thinks that even when and if the maps of the world change color, Ecuadorian attitudes toward the future may take a while longer to catch up. "Educated Ecuadorians," he says, "chuckle about U. S. culture and our belief that we can control things. From the Ecuadorian perspective, Americans ignore the many things they have no power over. There's some sense in thinking this way, when you live in a country with a strong or severe earthquake almost every decade, and where you're daily and inescapably surrounded by an extraordinarily dense concentration of volcanoes." Volcanoes are a recurring theme in Ecuadorian conversations. Gaus, bringing me up to speed one afternoon, said "uncertainty becomes the norm" and mentioned that Alexander von Humboldt, the great nineteenth-century German naturalist and traveler, coined the phrase "Avenue of the Volcanoes," still used today for the line of seven high, snow-capped peaks running south through Ecuador along the Andes for two hundred miles.

"There are fifty-five volcanoes in the country in all, seventeen of which might erupt at any moment," Gaus went on. "There's even a volcano called Sangay down in the eastern Ecuadorian Amazonian rainforest which has been in more or less continuous eruption since 1934, and the Galápagos Islands, out in the Pacific to the west of the mainland, are one of the world's most active volcanic hotspots. Just a couple of years ago, *Volcán* Wolf, the highest peak in the Galápagos, sent a plume of ash and gas nine and a half miles into the sky."

Gaus continued:

Quito wraps itself around the eastern slopes of a twin-peaked volcano, making it the only capital city in the world right next to an active volcano—which erupted, briefly and smokily— in 1999. I was here for that. The city got covered in several inches of ash.

At night *quiteños* can hear the sounds of the volcano coming from underground into their houses and apartments—it's like a stomach rumbling, they say. So maybe that's why Ecuadorians traditionally take a here-and-now approach to life, one that doesn't necessarily look ahead. Humboldt himself called Ecuadorians "strange and one-of-a kind," saying that they sleep calmly in the middle of "crunchy" volcanoes, live poor in the middle of incomparable riches, and cheer up when they hear sad music. I guess Humboldt found folk music lugubrious.

It's so complex, disentangling one part of life from another [Gaus said, going back to talking about health]. Ecuadorians are more forthright and accepting about death than we are, saying simply to expect it when the time comes. Maybe as disease becomes more of an occasional visitor to Ecuadorians, they may realize—if I take care of myself and only get sick intermittently, then that becomes something I can fix. And this can have a spillover effect. They might not have believed in prevention, the things you can do—exercise, eat right—because they were too cynical and skeptical and fatalistic about their health. Like the volcanoes, it was something over which they had no control. So putting a hospital in their lives is a way of handing them more control.

As in other Spanish-speaking countries, you hear the word "health"—*salud*—every day. It's a toast; it's what you say when someone sneezes; in a slightly different form it's the standard way to send respectful greetings. But when it became a politeness, it sounded like a wish, a someday thing, an aspiration rather than something available or already here. If Ecuadorians could come round to an outlook that's at least neutral about what could happen next or later on, and if it resulted in a lifting of worry, that would itself be a great step. Then they could think about lengthening lifespans and improving their health spans within a life, addressing what doctors think of as mortality and morbidity, which is a way of talking about staying alive but continuing to function well even in the face of ailments.

Mothers in Africa, according to one of Gaus's colleagues, often postpone giving "real names" to children until after they've survived measles, which on that continent still kills one infant every minute. Contrast that with the United States, where many people think the real purpose of your twenties is to have a decade to figure out what you want to do with your life. After this conversation with Gaus, I got a picture in my mind of life as sustained by health, a landscape at one's feet, not just a flickering expanse but a fully illuminated place, a long, mostly level ground extending indefinitely down clear sight lines, a kind of immortality within mortality.

CHAPTER TWO

"CAN YOU FIX HER?"

AT THE QUITO AIRPORT MY FIRST NIGHT IN ECUADOR, Gaus wedged Rosa the SimMom's carrying case into the back of a minivan. I'd already read a bit about medical simulation, which many educationalists—educators who study the effects of different types of education—think of as a crossover point in modern medical training at which proficiency is measured not by how much time you've spent studying something but by how competent you've become. Mastery of new skills, not memorization, is the goal.

Sim Med is more than just a way of fulfilling the old Hippocratic ideal embraced by every generation of doctors for more than two thousand years—"First, do no harm." But that's certainly part of it: The slogan of the Simulation Center at Johns Hopkins is "First, practice on plastic." Another part is reinforcement and feedback: A SimMom can be hooked up to a computer, and students and residents can record her actions for immediate video review the way football players study game films, although on a more urgent basis, since a SimMom can be programmed to present life-and-death medical emergencies.

Sim Med is also a way of stopping the clock in what had been an almost unvarying set of fast-moving expectations originally devised for training surgical residents a century ago, summed up in the well-known phrase "See one, do one, teach one" (where "one" is a real-life operation). Now it can be "See a sim operation, do one—and if necessary do another and another and maybe a dozen more—so that the procedures have entered your muscular memory before you ever face an actual patient, either as a practitioner or as a teacher. Simulation, says one academic overview, is still in its infancy but "is and will be pervasive" and will "persist for the next century." The practice of medicine will no longer mean practicing on a patient.

Simulation turns off the distraction of alarm bells and eases professionals into competence and confidence. U.S. Airways Captain Chesley Sullenberger III, the man responsible for the "Miracle on the Hudson"—who in January 2009 landed his plane on the Hudson River, the only wide-open space in the middle of New York City, after multiple bird strikes three minutes into his flight had crippled both his engines, and then successfully evacuated all 155 people on board—attributed much of his calmness during the emergency to simulation training. A member of the National Transportation Safety Board called it "the most successful ditching in aviation history," adding, "These people knew what they were supposed to do, and they did it." "Sully," the captain's nickname and the title of a 2016 movie about him starring Tom Hanks, said of the experience: "For forty-two years, I've been making small, regular deposits in this bank of experience, education, and training. And on January 15 the balance was sufficient so that I could make a very large withdrawal."

Almost one hundred years of concentrated thinking about getting better at doing things was entering Ecuador with Rosa. I learned more about this later, on a field trip that David Gaus arranged for me, to the State University of New York (SUNY)–

Downstate Medical Center, a large medical school and hospital in Brooklyn, New York. The medical school has a $900 million annual operating budget and treats over ninety thousand patients a year, and Sim Med has been hugely effective for training a truly megadiverse group of students and residents—ninety-three languages are spoken in Brooklyn, sixty of them at SUNY–Downstate, and for 43 percent of first-year med students, English is their second language. The president of the medical center was a member of Gaus's advisory board.

Dr. Margaret Clifton, a SUNY–Downstate nurse educator and director of the sim lab, walked me through the remarkably cheerful, blond-wood-paneled, softly skylighted, spacious facility; over each bed there are murals of tree leaves. The full history of simulation, she told me, traces back two thousand years, to Roman gladiators, who practiced with wooden swords. The first specially designed piece of modern sim machinery, invented in 1929, was the Link Trainer, also known as the Blue Box because it resembled a cramped, stubby, windowless, blue-painted airplane. It helped pilots in the early years of commercial aviation get used to thinking counterintuitively, learning to trust that in bad weather, when the ground was obscured by fog or rain, they could rely on on-board instruments. Half a million U.S. military pilots prepared for missions on Link Trainers during World War II.

Medical simulation began in 1960, when Laerdal, the Norwegian company that now makes SimMom and previously had made rubber toy cars, introduced "Resusci Anne," sometimes called "CPR Annie," a half-manikin, to teach chest compressions and mouth-to-mouth resuscitation, at that time a new technique for reviving someone in cardiac arrest. The head of the company, Asmund Laerdal, who'd saved his own son from drowning, gave the manikin the hauntingly beautiful, smiling face of a nineteenth-century Parisian girl who'd drowned in the Seine—an image preserved as a death mask. Laerdal thought emergency medical technician students would be "better motivated to learn" if they saw her face, now called "the most kissed face of all time."

Hi-fi manikins like Rosa—"hi-fi" meaning they have breathing sounds and heart rhythms that can crash and die—emerged in the 1990s, and sim labs can "debrief the feelings" as well as the actions of the students. "When SimMan or SimMom dies," Dr. Clifton said, "he or she will be back tomorrow. But the first time students see him or her die, maybe because somebody forgot to watch the monitor, they're very emotionally involved. It's an opportunity to talk immediately afterwards about the passion that brought them to healing."

The new Quito airport is twenty-one miles from downtown, and much of the roadway is winding. On the long drive, I had questions for Gaus about Rosa. How difficult had it been bringing her through customs as checked luggage, and what role would she take on now that she was cleared to stay in the country?

Characteristically, his answers covered a lot of different ground:

Well, I was trying to speed things along. It would've cost an arm and a leg to have a manikin sent, and you never know what shape it'll be in by the time it gets here. I also need it right away because we have new residents coming and we're starting a course soon. But a SimMom is something the customs people had never seen before; it looked weird to them. Well, it *does* look weird. So they asked a lot of questions, like was I a doctor, and who do I work with, and what were they looking at, and would I be selling it, and why shouldn't they charge me for it? I started off telling them what a good job they're doing and how happy it made me that they were being so careful about putting the brakes on illegal stuff. I told them I'm working with a very poor population in the countryside, that I'm part of a movement to do this, and it's a great opportunity to teach Ecuadorians how to take care of their fellow citizens. I was very polite, very kind. A lot of it's just being respectful. In Ecuador, *respeto*—respect—is probably the key ingredient in all encounters, and of course you show respect for someone by taking an interest in what they're doing. The flip side is when my typical U.S. side comes out, and I have to keep an eye on that. In the States, if you're a dog who won't let go of a bone, your attitude is applauded. If you're having trouble with an agency or a group, just pile in and blast forward. Whereas in Ecuador you have to learn when to accept a *no* and quit leaving a trail of wounded behind you.

Rosa is going to be helpful in several ways, but you do understand, she's just one piece of how we're shaping family physicians for work in the countryside. Ecuadorians like novelty stuff, and Sim Med is fascinating. It strengthens and speeds up all kinds of learning, even more so than many of the other Johnny-come-lately techniques. So, sure, there's a part of Rosa that's as simple as the fact that I can show people a state-of-the-art technology that even Quito barely has, so maybe some doctors will quit turning up their noses at the idea of a career in a rural area. It meant a lot to us when we opened our Clínica de Simulación Médica and got good local radio and TV coverage.

But with or without Rosa, what we're really coming to grips with is a deep-seated need to reduce maternal mortality from birth complications. There's a lot of it, way too much in the countryside, and no specialists, so it's something a general practitioner or a family medicine M.D. has to be able to handle. Our cry has been for Ecuadorian medical schools to build some sort of competency into their curriculum. The Ecuadorian Ministry of Public Health has been working hard to address this issue, but the infant mortality rate is three times higher than in, say, Wisconsin; maternal mortality is more than seven and a half times higher. The probability that a teenage mother will die from some kind of pregnancy complication is one in 150 in developing countries, one in 3,800 in the developed world. Local doctors need to practice on and get comfortable with the emergencies that will come up and be absolutely prepared.

That way doctors won't run out the back door for lunch when an emergency is brought in the front door—which actually happened to my closest partner, Dr. Diego Herrera, now AHD's director. Years ago, Diego was the attending physician at Hospital Pedro Vicente Maldonado when an emergency came in. There were three other health care personnel alongside Diego, and all four were needed. Suddenly, after two minutes, the other three were gone. Later that day they confessed they thought the patient was going to die and they wanted no part of having to face the family. The thing is, in emergencies, you only have so much time. There's a concept known as the "Golden Hour," meaning the short period available—it can be as little as thirty minutes—when prompt medical attention can stabilize someone's condition and prevent death.

In a pregnancy, one of the most frightening, life-threatening conditions is called eclampsia. This means sudden, convulsive seizures during or before childbirth, and its 2,500-year-old name is itself a description of how scary it is, a Greek word that means a sudden flashing or lightning bolt, or a bolt from the blue. Seizures usually last about a minute. There are violent shakings; the eyes roll back, the jaw clamps. Then there's a period of confusion or coma, which can be followed by death.

Supposedly the name was coined by Hippocrates, and it's the result of a placenta that doesn't function properly, though even today no one quite knows the how or the why of it. We do know that its warning signs—preeclampsia—often develop around the sixth month of a pregnancy, marked by high blood pressure, protein in the urine, and maybe swelling in the feet and legs, and weight gain of more than two pounds a week. We've known for a hundred years that seizures can be treated and prevented by injections of magnesium sulfate, otherwise known as Epsom salts, though again it's still not clear why this is effective—and Epsom salts were themselves an accidental discovery two hundred years before that, when a farmer in Epsom, England, noticed that his cows wouldn't drink from a certain well but the bitter water seemed to heal rashes and scratches. Magnesium sulfate, old and inexpensive as it is, often can't be found in Ecuadorian health care facilities when it can so easily save a life.

Culturally, many Ecuadorian women still prefer delivering at home. We need to get women into the hospital—first for a checkup during pregnancy, and then to have the baby. I know there are profound cultural reservations to work through, having heard Ecuadorian fathers asking, why is a white man from Quito putting his hands into my wife's private parts? It's another complex, tip-of-the-iceberg situation, because if the families don't come to us, then we'll never know what they're sick and dying from, and they can so easily become tragic examples of incidents that rarely get public attention but that people here live with, have always lived with. The best guess we have is that between 10 and 25 percent of rural women who develop preeclampsia will die.

In 1997, several months after I got back to Ecuador, before we built the first hospital and when I was just running a small rural clinic, a young man we'd never seen before carried his 24-year-old wife, Carmen, into the office, his young son holding onto his dad's pants pocket. Two weeks before her due date, Carmen had seized at home and died after bleeding in her head. The young man hadn't yet taken any of this in. "She fell asleep," he said. "Can you fix her?"

There was a silence. For most of the long ride Gaus and I had been in darkness; now, as we approached downtown Quito, the inside of the car had become visible in the bright streetlights around us. I'd been sitting in the front, taking notes, and I turned to look at Gaus. There were tears in his eyes as he talked about a baby he hadn't been able to save and a woman he hadn't been able to help, twenty years before.

CHAPTER THREE

CAMINO A LA CURA

BEFORE GOING TO BED IN A QUITO HOTEL, WHERE WE'D be briefly—we were heading down to Gaus's hospitals early in the morning, after a quick drive through the historic heart of Quito—I had a David Foster Wallace fish-out-of-water moment in which I caught a glimpse of what it would be like *not* to be constantly encircled and buoyed by health. It was nothing that hasn't happened to great numbers of North American travelers in the developing world, but it stayed with me because it was late, because I was in a new place, because of what Gaus and I had been talking about. Oh, and because of the ordinariness of it. I was brushing my teeth.

Before saying goodnight, and in the middle of going over the next day's timetable, David Gaus had casually remarked that as long as I was in Ecuador, I should make sure to use only bottled water from a sealed bottle when brushing my teeth and to keep my mouth shut when taking a shower. And to never eat peeled fruit unless I peeled it myself. Pretty standard warnings for North Americans abroad. It's somewhat awkward and requires thought to rinse a toothbrush with a dribble of water from a bottle, though probably the worst that would've happened (if I'd used faucet water by mistake) would've been a couple of days with an upset stomach. And anyway I was traveling with Dr. Gaus, who would've known what to do about it.

But the uncomfortableness of having to pay attention to something you always do automatically can bring up a more consequential question: What's your strategy for health when, no matter what you do, how much attention you pay, it's normal to expect things to go wrong, and there will only be a limited number of things you can do that may or may not make everything right?

As I learned after talking to some of Gaus's patients, Ecuadorians without a lot of money have evolved an informal, not-so-safe safety net, one that an Ecuadorian medical anthropologist calls the *camino a la cura*, the road or pathway to a cure. It begins, as in many U.S. households, with remedies that mothers and grandmothers swear by and always have handy—although Ecuadorian women, no doubt partly from necessity, seem to have a far greater range of substances put aside that just might work.

According to "13 Signs You Were Born and Raised by an Ecuadorian Mother," a vivid online article by Jess López, a young Ecuadorian writer and environmentalist, "Your house was a sort of alternative medicine repository," because "there is a combination of natural herbs for each condition and only moms know which is which." Some of the recipes López grew up with, along with Vick's VapoRub and cod liver oil, included an egg's inner membrane, useful for healing scars; a 50-cent piece, which "cured bumps"; "a cold padlock," which "(after leaving it out overnight) will treat a stye." There were also "thousands of other herbs, teas, and beverages you never managed to identify or name, yet found themselves in the medicine cabinet." All had to be taken *sin respirar y sin chistar*—without pausing for a breath, without making a sound, without back-talk. Eating was especially important. "The sick who eat," her grandmother would say, "do not die."

If whatever was wrong didn't respond to the treatment of a mom or an *abuela*, a grandmother, the next step meant leaving the house and spending money. There might be a visit to a *curandero*—an indigenous shaman; those from the Tsáchila people near Santo Domingo have a reputation as the most powerful healers. Massage is also widely considered effective as a therapeutic treatment, and masseuses are found throughout the country, even in small towns. What if that doesn't work either? Well, practically every town also has at least one *farmacia*, where almost any drug is available without prescription, and pharmacists routinely do an excellent business diagnosing and prescribing, though they are just local businessmen with no special training as druggists.

Finally, Gaus says:

> When you're all out of money, you may try a Western-trained doctor who graduated from an Ecuadorian med school. The whole *camino* is a pathway designed to avoid contact with the country's established walk-in clinic and hospital system— they have the reputation U.S. hospitals had a century ago, as cold, dark, dirty places where people go to die. The *camino* does a reasonably good job as a detour or bypass road. The problem comes if there's something life-threatening going on. The Western-trained physicians, if they're turned to, will assume it's likely that various remedies have been tried and that there may have been some complications and consequences from these treatments—which further confuses the picture.

Whenever something life-threatening does arise in any town without even a rudimentary hospital, there's a truly harrowing further extension to the *camino a la cura*. This one involves a real *camino*—the long drives on the highway that desperate people have to make, usually in a pickup truck, from the countryside up into the mountains, and then taking their chances at a public hospital in the capital. Seared into Gaus's mind are memories of rural families for whom that final trip brought only heartache.

One such family was that of 17-year-old Isabel (Gaus remembers names, too), who saw three doctors before being told she had appendicitis. Because her town had no surgical facilities, she was driven to Quito, arriving only to die there from a ruptured appendix. Gustavo, 43, was in a truck crash and broke one of his "long bones," as doctors call the bones in the legs and arms. There were no orthopedists in his town to set his femur, and he was taken to Quito—or toward Quito, because on the way he bled to death inside his own leg.

A farm worker, 28-year-old Vicente, always wore his standard outfit of shorts, a tank top, and flip-flops when spraying *chontaduro* palm trees—crunchy "hearts of palm" are cut from them. On his back he carried a tank of insecticide, and he walked through thick clouds of the stuff; in the United States he would've been wearing something that looked like a moon suit. He developed a serious organophosphate intoxication. Organophosphates were developed in the 1930s by a German chemist who wanted to fight world hunger with better pesticides, but Hitler's military converted the chemicals into nerve gases; both uses persist. Organophosphates block an enzyme critical to nerve function in humans and insects alike and can be absorbed through the lungs or the skin. Vicente was having trouble breathing, but there were no ventilators in his town. He, too, was taken to Quito and actually got there, but sat unnoticed in an emergency room hallway until he died of lung failure.

CHAPTER FOUR

A BEGGAR SITTING
ON A BAG OF GOLD

ECUADOR IS APPROXIMATELY THE SIZE OF COLORADO, and, like Colorado, would be a lot bigger if it could be flattened out. Both places are bisected from north to south by tall mountain chains, but the Ecuadorian Andes are a mile higher than Colorado's Front Range Rockies, and when you head east off the Andes you find yourself in the still largely unexplored upper reaches of the Amazon basin and its rainforest, while in many places to the west the Pacific Ocean is no more than 150 miles away.

In addition to having terrain that in cross-section rises from sea level to over twenty-one thousand feet (a glacier-topped volcano called Chimborazo is the highest point of all) and then sinks back down to less than five hundred feet in the Amazonian region, Ecuador is draped across the Equator ("Ecuador" is Spanish for the Equator) and sits on two continental plates, which, some twelve miles or more underground, are slowly but inexorably scraping across each other. They move at the rate of only about three inches a year, but this is fast enough to account for the many earthquakes and volcanoes in the country.

Long before humanity arrived, two fundamental traits of the country had already been established: profuse abundance in the midst of unending precariousness. It's thought that tropical sun and temperatures generate new species and adaptations faster than cooler climates—for biologists the tag line is a variant of a phrase from Lewis Carroll's *Through the Looking-Glass*, "The Red Queen runs faster when she is hot." The country's hump-backed bell curve of land elevations has allowed for a compact layering or stacking up of natural plenty, since often you can pass from one ecosystem to another simply by moving 100 feet up or down a single hillside.

This makes Ecuador what's called a "megadiverse" country—with, for instance, six thousand species of butterflies, more species of birds than in the United States and Europe combined, and forty-two hundred species of orchids, including something called the Monkey Face Orchid, which seems to have two dark, soulful, close-set eyes above a pinched nose and an open mouth, and which, for reasons equally mysterious, smells like an orange. Altogether there's more biodiversity per square mile here than in any other country, with about a million species or more than a tenth of the total species in the world.

At the beginning of the nineteenth century, the dazzling range of life on display here left such a deep impression on Alexander von Humboldt that it inspired his masterwork, five volumes about the essential unity and order of the universe, which he finished on his 89th birthday. Reading one of Humboldt's earlier books, the young Charles Darwin was himself inspired to travel to South America—and it was in Ecuador's Galápagos Islands, as the world knows, that his own careful observations of changes within species laid the groundwork for his theory of evolution.

Human life in Ecuador plays out against this spectacular natural backdrop—and, as in many other countries, *against* is the operative word, in that the two realms often exist in isolation from or at odds with each other. Ecuador is one of the five poorest countries in South America; as Humboldt said more than two hundred years ago, its people live poor in the midst of incomparable riches. It's also one of the smallest South American nations—both of the countries next door, Colombia and Peru, have more people and bigger economies, and each is twice the size of Texas. Just to the east is Brazil, larger than the forty-eight contiguous U.S. states put together and widely seen as an emerging superpower. Nevertheless, Ecuador is the most densely populated country in South America; less than five percent of its sixteen million people live in the *Oriente*, the Amazonian East, and everybody else is in the central mountains, on the seacoast, or in the forest-turned-farmland in between.

In some ways Ecuador is a rich nation in disguise, or in waiting. Poverty, though still an inescapable reality, is no longer quite the stark presence it once was. Statistics show it continuously decreasing since 1999—affecting half the country then and about a quarter of it now. Anti-poverty progress has accelerated since the populist administration of former president Rafael Correa, who took office in 2007 and launched its "citizens' revolution," which some call "oil socialism" and others call "extractivism," meaning drilling for oil in virgin Amazonian rainforest. Oil was discovered in Ecuador in 1967; along with Venezuela, it's one of two Western Hemisphere members of OPEC (the Organization of Petroleum Exporting Countries).

By the end of its first nine years, the citizens' revolution had redirected $7.5 billion of oil revenues, previously used to pay off the national debt, into a massive and unusually ambitious public works program, building hundreds of new schools and thousands of miles of new roads, cutting unemployment in half, and making primary school education free for all while also hiking the minimum wage by 80 percent. One and a half million Ecuadorians emerged from poverty as a result, with the number of people living in extreme poverty (defined as existing on $1.25 a day) falling by half. In 2015 Correa tweeted—like so many current world leaders, Correa tweets—that the country had successfully transformed its oil richness into greater well-being for all. Correa, an American-trained economist with a Belgian wife, often quotes Humboldt's line about Ecuador's being a beggar sitting on a bag of gold.

Driving along new roads through the suburbs of Quito, you come across just-opened shopping centers and brand-new, pastel-tinted, gated townhouse communities. Out on these roads the citizens' revolution takes on an oddly hybrid but very North American flavor, as if Franklin D. Roosevelt's array of Depression-era New Deal programs had been delayed by a generation so they could incorporate the Eisenhower administration's postwar creation of the U. S. Interstate highway system.

Another postwar touch—this one from the 1960s, not the 1950s—is a *Mad Men*–style public relations campaign waged by the government on behalf of the citizens' revolution on large roadside billboards featuring splashy graphics, bright colors, and brief, drive-by glimpses of future prosperity, all under the hopeful slogan *Ecuador ya cambió!* (Ecuador has already changed!). On one of these posters, three men look ahead to careers they might choose: one has a stethoscope, another a microscope, and the third holds the protons-and-whirling-electrons symbol of an atom.

David Gaus looks past the billboards and, not surprisingly, focuses on several things other people might overlook. The Correa administration, for example, takes pride in having doubled per capita spending on health care and on the construction of dozens of new outpatient clinics and hospitals, but Gaus suspects that the government's poverty reduction efforts may have a more direct and more lasting impact on national health—he invokes what's called the "McKeown Thesis" or the "McKeown Hypothesis."

The reference here is to Thomas McKeown, a twentieth-century British physician and professor of social medicine. In 1975 McKeown noticed that nineteenth- and twentieth-century English health care data revealed, contrary to what had been expected, that death rates from a number of highly contagious infectious diseases, including bronchitis, pneumonia, and the flu, had begun a sharp decline decades before antibiotics, antiviral drugs, and other medicines became available. McKeown graphed a similarly precipitous drop in TB deaths, showing that the decline began a century before modern treatments and even predated by 45 years the epochal 1882 discovery of TB's causative agent, the tuberculosis bacillus, by Robert Koch, later a Nobel Prize winner and now acknowledged as the "Father of Bacteriology." McKeown attributed this to an overlooked upside of the Industrial Revolution: Workers with steady factory jobs had rising standards of living and could afford better food, which reduced exposure to infections and built up greater resistance to them. The McKeown Hypothesis has been challenged but has also found broad support. Robert Fogel, a Nobel Economics Prize winner who agrees with the McKeown Hypothesis, has suggested that "about 40 percent of the decline in mortality is due to improved nutrition."

Gaus also finds himself sustained by something humbler but far more ubiquitous than billboards: In almost every town or wayside village, the square cinderblock pillars that support the one- and two-story houses lining the streets extend for several feet beyond the flat roofs and have rusty steel reinforcing poles, called rebar, sprouting from their tops. At first you wonder if these are lightning rods or homemade TV antennas or maybe spikes designed to keep birds from landing. According to Gaus, they're a set of national aspirations, announcing that even a fully occupied building is still unfinished, at least in its owner's mind. There's a law on the books that defers property taxes on buildings still under construction, so maybe the rebar is actually aimed at tax collectors. But Gaus sees something deeper at play. He calls the rebar "Ecuadorian hope."

Gaus points out that what haven't declined are the needs of rural people. Rural poverty has been a far more persistent statistic than poverty in the aggregate and now stands at 42 percent. Officially the overall rural population is in retreat and amounts to no more than a third of the country; this seems to echo the historic global trend toward urbanization—the United Nations found that in 2009, for the first time in human history, more people around the world lived in urban areas than in rural ones. But, in Ecuador at least, the urban population percentages fail to give proper weight, or even take into account, a more slowly moving but all-important reality, a phenomenon called "rurality," which refers to "a place at the interface between rural and urban" that's not necessarily "within the influence of a metropolitan area." For Gaus and Herrera, this is a way of describing the Ecuadorian fact that only the inhabitants of the two largest cities, Guayaquil and Quito, have a full range of big-city institutions they can count on or, for that matter, have come to think of themselves as city people.

Gaus says:

> In Ecuador, there are two worlds. Quito and Guayaquil are urban and Western-oriented. The other is the traditional *mestizaje* world. This refers to people of combined European and Amerindian descent, who make up over 70 percent of the country, and to a mindset of modernity with elements of an older Amerindian world view. But living more closely together, as they do in Santo, doesn't change people overnight. By the revised math here, three-quarters of the people are still rural by location or rural at heart—even as they struggle toward modernity. And still subject to deprivations in health services by a system that does not understand them very well.

There's also a buried heartache and sting in Ecuadorian life that dates back centuries. There are eight hundred acres at the heart of Quito, defined by their steep, narrow streets and five thousand buildings—a stunning assemblage of small, jewel-box-sized, tile-roofed houses, elegant palaces, and exquisite, gold-leaf-adorned churches, some dating back to the sixteenth century, whose architecture is considered a unique fusion of Spanish, Italian, Moorish, Flemish, and indigenous American traditions. In 1978 these eight hundred acres were inscribed in UNESCO's list of World Heritage sites (one of the first two cities in the world to achieve this honor), where they were singled out as "the best-preserved, least altered historic center in Latin America." (UNESCO is the United Nations Educational, Scientific, and Cultural Organization.)

What the UNESCO citation doesn't mention is that, for more than a century, after fashionable *quiteños* had abandoned the area as old-fashioned, it became the city's red-light district. In polite society this relegated it to the status of an off-limits place whose existence still had to be acknowledged and tolerated but otherwise would rarely be mentioned—and certainly wouldn't appear in planning documents.

Quito's old downtown is built on the obliterated ruins of the Incan city of Quito, which the Incans burned in 1533 rather than letting them fall into the hands of Spanish invaders. Only the name remains, but the greatest wound of that time was the one inadvertently inflicted on Ecuadorians during the Spanish conquest in that decade, so that the founding of Ecuador was also a foundering—a profound human tragedy and unprecedented health catastrophe that, had it been intended, would have amounted to germ warfare.

Before Columbus set sail across the Atlantic in 1492, the New World had been an isolated hemisphere with its own unique array of plants and animals. The Spanish who followed him brought along (to name just a few) cows, chickens, horses, apples, coffee, bananas, wheat, and rice and took home turkeys, cocoa, blueberries, pineapples, potatoes, tobacco, and tomatoes.

There were invisible pathological participants in this otherwise benign "Columbian Exchange," as historians call it—more than a dozen Old World infectious diseases, including smallpox and measles, which Europeans had acquired some immunity to but that so devastated American populations, both North and South, they were practically exterminated almost overnight.

Estimates vary as to the extent of the losses, but up to 90 percent of many communities succumbed. Death on this scale and with this suddenness brought with it a shattering cultural implosion and a jagged discontinuity with nearly everything that had gone before. "So thorough was the erasure," Charles C. Mann says in *1491*, his eye-opening book about the life in the Americas that had disappeared so abruptly, "that within a few generations neither conqueror nor conquered knew that this world had existed."

We know very little about the health enjoyed by Ecuadorians before the Spanish arrived, although Theodor Wolf, the distinguished German naturalist who made the first definitive survey of the Galápagos in the late nineteenth century, is on record as saying that "there are few tropical countries in the world as good or as healthy for the human species as Ecuador, as far as the climate is concerned."

Did anything survive? In Ecuador, where the Incas themselves were newcomers who had arrived only a century before the Spanish, the only physical remains of their presence are one castle and isolated segments of the Royal Road they built along the Andes from Quito to Argentina. But if you know where to look or listen, here and there you can detect haunting traces of a shaken and subjected society trying to come to terms with immeasurable loss.

One such reverberation is embedded in everyday language. Gaus noticed it early on, when he was still mastering Spanish himself, and looked into the reason behind what sounded like no more than a stylistic archaic formulation: "Ever since the Spanish conquest of the Inca Empire," he told me, "people here don't say, 'I dropped the glass,' but rather, 'The glass fell out of my hand.' The indigenous people who didn't perish knew they'd get blamed for everything that went wrong, so they removed themselves from the conversation and learned to use words that avoided any hint of blame. It became an established, pervasive way of speaking. Now, at least to hear people talk, nobody actually *does* anything. Instead things just happen."

Another manifestation shows up in the specialized, colorful costumes and adornments of a particular group of indigenous Ecuadorians, the pre-Incan Tsáchila people, the group whose shamans are held in such respect. Their remaining lands are not far from Santo Domingo, and the larger province that includes the city gets its name from them: Santo Domingo de los Tsáchilas.

The Tsáchilas had to endure the long-ago Spanish conquest and the more recent, more benevolent impulses of a mid-twentieth-century Ecuadorian president. The president conferred big plots of forestland on them at a time that they might have been displaced altogether by land-clearing settlers, but he insisted on chopping up the land in a checkerboard pattern, thinking this would integrate the Tsáchilas into modern society. These pieces of land, though now protected, further fragmented and isolated the Tsáchila communities, converting their ancestral stronghold into something more like a series of "weakholds." Their numbers are small—no more than twenty-eight hundred in all—but they persist and, if you know how to read the clues, as Gaus and his colleagues have learned to do, even their appearance is a defiant, health-affirming statement, one that proclaims their indomitability.

The most striking thing about Tsáchila men is their hairstyle: they shave their heads up to the crown, and then use grease to form the long hair on top into a kind of leaf-shaped helmet, pointed in the front and dyed bright red with seeds from the achiote bush, native to tropical South America and sometimes called the "lipstick tree." (Achiote seeds were part of the "Columbian Exchange," and in the 1500s, in a more deceitful kind of symbolism, some English cheese makers used them to make inferior white cheese look more like butterfat-rich yellow cheese; the supermarket descendant of these efforts is Velveeta.)

The Tsáchila headdress resembles an achiote leaf, and, according to tradition, when a postconquest smallpox epidemic struck the community, which originally lived higher in the Andes, a spirit told a Tsáchila shaman to cover everyone from head to toe with red juice from achiote seeds. Several days later, the smallpox deaths dramatically decreased. The headdresses are a way of continuing to give thanks, and also of saying, "Never forget." Today the men still paint black horizontal lines across their faces and wear dark-blue skirts striped with thin black horizontal lines. The black lines, they say, protect against negative energy and honor ancestors "who died from introduced diseases," while the skirts are supposed to ward off bites from an *equis*—Spanish for "X" and the local name for the fer-de-lance, a large and venomous pit viper whose body is cross-hatched with X-like markings.

This is the country where David Gaus and his team have set up shop, working to create conditions that can establish health as one of its greatest treasures. It's a country whose natural assets are spectacular, even superlative—and vulnerable at all times to widespread destruction by earthquakes and volcanoes. Age-old social problems are being tackled through twenty-first-century government spending, but the pace of these changes is itself vulnerable, since so many recent improvements depend on the fluctuating market price of the oil the country pumps from the Amazonian rainforest.

The most persistent forces in the country are the deprivation that still shadows the lives of so many people in the countryside and the enduring presence of Ecuadorian hope—which, beyond the gaudy roadside billboards and the rebar sticking out of rooftops—may have found a home in the city that is not yet a city that had attracted David Gaus's attention several years back: Santo Domingo de los Colorados, which means "red-colored"; the city's full name, like that of the larger province around it, honors the Tsáchila people.

CHAPTER FIVE

TRANSISTOR
RADIOS

THE STORY OF SANTO DOMINGO—AT LEAST SO FAR—IS IN many ways the story of Hólger Velasteguí, an enterprising radio station owner who over fifty years ago became the then-tiny community's tireless well-wisher and Pied Piper. When still in his twenties, Velasteguí, who'd been born in a small Andean village south of Quito and had worked his way through college as a radio announcer, looked at the World Bank plans for Ecuador's first highway-building program. The roads were going to link the Pacific coast and the mountains, which it called "antagonistic regions," in the process "opening up vast tracts of land to new settlement." Velasteguí realized that two of the four roads would intersect in Santo, making it *"la tierra de promisión del Ecuador,"* or Ecuador's promised land, once the forests—then considered to be only *tierras baldías*, meaning vain, useless, pointless, unutilized lands, were felled for banana plantations and cattle ranches.

When Velasteguí's radio station went on the air in 1959, he had to rent a generator, because the town, which then had a single unpaved street, also had no electricity. But the station caught on because, after Velasteguí asked people what they wanted to hear, it broadcast Ecuadorian folk music almost exclusively (the kind Humboldt found so dreary and gloomy). And because Velasteguí, in a pre-Internet world, himself read the news out loud on air (back then it took a day or more for Quito newspapers to make their way to the countryside). And also because for 50 cents or less you could get the station to run a *comunicado*, a short personal or family message, usually at mealtimes; *comunicados* acted as a kind of regionwide texting service at a time when almost no one had landline phones.

What people did have were transistor radios. They were just then becoming the most popular piece of electronic equipment ever invented, so that all around the country—and even in southern Colombia, a seven-hour drive to the north—people heard Velasteguí tell his listeners, as a wandering *New York Times* writer later reported, that "the land was rich and the people good" and this was where "those with a dream" should come. People came. From farms near Loja, one of the oldest cities in the country (the first one wired for electricity), which sits in the "Valley of Smiles," which had been suffering a prolonged drought. From farms in El Oro, the southernmost province that borders Peru, and from *minifundios* (smallholdings) in Manabi, a coastal province, both of which had been having bad droughts of their own.

Those farmers were joined by unemployed workers from Quito and Guayaquil, and also by Colombians fleeing *la violencia*, the country's longest continuous war, a brutal four-sided conflict dating back to 1948—among government troops, leftist guerillas, narco cartels, and right-wing paramilitaries—that has killed more than a quarter of a million people and displaced more than six million, either within the country or abroad. A peace agreement with the main guerilla group was finally ratified by the Colombian Congress in November 2016.

So many displaced Colombians wound up in Santo that they started calling it Santo Domingo de los Colombianos (rather than Santo Domingo de los Colorados). "I heard all about this place," a former Colombian told the *Times* writer, "even in my little town back home. You do not miss your country here."

This national—and international—group thrown together at the new crossroads of what had always been deep country-side turned Santo and its surroundings into the *despensa nacional*, the national pantry, as Velasteguí called it. It's also a "terrestrial port," an exchange point for goods moving between the highlands and the coast. These resettlers, farmers, shopkeepers, truckers, and middlemen also forged new associations, setting up agricultural and housing cooperatives, and eventually became an unofficial and novel factor in Ecuadorian society, one that Velasteguí hailed as the "*crisol de la nacionalidad ecuatoriana*"—the crucible of Ecuadorian nationality.

Common need and opportunity have proved stronger than fiercely held inherited rivalries between mountain people and coastal people and have even softened Ecuadorians' longtime suspiciousness of "violent" Colombians (a legacy of that country's civil war and drug wars).

Lost along the way were mile after mile of forests, forests probably teeming with biodiversity but dismissed as wastelands by pre-ecological thinking. The Tsáchila, dependent on these forests, were further marginalized, though at the same time held up as heroic figures—Velasteguí's station is named Radio Zaracay, after Joaquin Zaracay, a beloved governor of the Tsáchila people.

Santo is still not much to look at—to a visitor it seems all outskirts with no center; you keep turning the corner expecting to see something different and see only more of the same—a lot of narrow, bustling streets lined by two- and three-story buildings, many with small shops or restaurants at ground level (and yes, with rebar sticking out of the roofs). The most elaborate pieces of civic design are several large traffic circles you have to dodge your way across. One of them has illuminated water jets in the middle. There's a miniature central park that's not very central and is named, perhaps inevitably, Zaracay Park. Hólgar Velasteguí, who eventually became the city's mayor, adorned it, perhaps also inevitably, with a Tsáchila monument, this one to Zaracay's successor as governor. There's only one unbuilt-on natural feature left in Santo, a hill in the northwest. The city is constantly noisy; it's hot and humid twelve months a year, and crime is a problem. A guide book for North Americans complains that getting to and from Santo "is far easier than finding anything to do once you're there."

But in a new place new things can be tried out, and tried more often than in other places, and perhaps then have a better chance of succeeding. This is not a bad definition of hope.

CHAPTER SIX

PANAMA HATS

THIS BASTION OF HOPE AND OUTPOST OF HEALTH WAS just where we were heading. Even with plenty of information on hand, it was hard to know exactly what I might get to see or how much would be on display, because nearly everything happening in Santo has been "off camera," so to speak. It isn't only North Americans who haven't heard about it—the *New York Times* report about Santo was a one-off with no follow-up visits. Because of its geological vulnerability, disasters and tragedies implacably strike the country, such as, most recently, the 7.8-magnitude earthquake that began twelve miles underground and shook the northwest coast on April 16, 2016, with as much power as the 1906 San Francisco earthquake had exhibited, killing 673 people and displacing 73,000 others. Events like these focus intense outside attention on the country as a whole, but only for weeks at a time. *Quiteños* and *guayaquileños* and other locals know next to nothing about their country's third-largest city, a situation that creates problems for Gaus and his colleagues.

These days outsiders can stay in close visual touch with places around the world, including the North Pole, which has live webcams during the summer months when the sun is constantly above the horizon, and Antarctica, where a research station has several penguin cams. In Ecuador, though, information can be somewhat more oblique. For instance, because of what might on any day start happening five or ten or twenty miles underground, cameras are trained on a small but breathtaking slice of the country's surface. The *Instituto Geofísico*, the national research center for earthquakes and volcanoes, has set up a network of nine webcams close to *Volcán* Cotopaxi, a majestic, glacier-capped, symmetrically conical volcano (like Mt. Fuji in Japan) thirty miles south of Quito. Partly because of the glacier ringing its peak, it's considered one of the most dangerous volcanoes in the world. In August 2015 it started emitting plumes of smoke and ash; in early September these plumes rose two and a half miles above the peak, reaching an altitude used by commercial airplanes.

The real danger of a full-blown Cotopaxi eruption, however, would be on the ground, not in the sky. It would create lahars, which are fast-moving torrents that combine lava and debris with mudslides caused by melted glacial ice. Lahars from an 1877 eruption actually poured downslope with such force that they reached the Pacific Ocean, a distance of 140 miles.

Only three of the Cotopaxi webcams show the mountain itself, often swathed in swirling mists and clouds like a Turner painting. The other six are trained on remote, steep, narrow, peaceful valleys that one day—if seismologists are right that a similar Cotopaxi blast is already overdue—may once again become lahars.

When not in Ecuador I find myself checking these webcams, because even at a remove, strong echoes of life in the Ecuadorian countryside come pulsing through. My personal favorite is one focused on a particular edge-of-town valley. It offers glimpses of buildings—a large factory or warehouse off in the background up on top of the far slope, with trees and grasses nearer by, which stay put while people, cars, trucks, and animals flicker in and out of view, a fleeting presence. This happens because the cameras are actually only almost-live—what they show is not quite streaming but repeated sequences of eleven still images shot over various five-minute intervals. Sometimes, but only sometimes, horses or cows appear, disappear, and reappear as they move around pastureland at the bottom of the valley. Sometimes a pig sticks its head out of a tidy, cinder-block pigpen at the top of the near slope.

Despite the fact that visiting the Galápagos Islands pops up on many people's bucket lists, comparatively few *norteamericanos* visit Ecuador at all—285,000 in 2012 versus almost 20 million who went to Mexico. Historically, some outlandish story will occasionally burst out of Ecuador and leave a lingering impression.

Back before World War II, *Off with Their Heads*, a book by Victor Wolfgang von Hagen, a wildly prolific explorer and travel writer from St. Louis (he wrote forty-six books), popularized the idea of eastern Ecuador as home base for an Amazonian tribe that shrank its enemies' heads. This story persists to a certain extent; the tribe in question, the Shuar people, long ago became Christian converts and conservationists and now serve with distinction in the national army. But as George Lauderbaugh, one of the few foreign historians inducted into Ecuador's National Academy of History, has pointed out, gift shops around the country still stock souvenir "faux shrunken heads" (which sell well).

Thirty-five years after von Hagen's book was published, a *National Geographic* cover story by a Harvard Medical School doctor claimed that villagers in Vilcabamba, an exceptionally beautiful Andean village in southernmost Ecuador, routinely lived to be 120 or older because, it was suggested, the fruit grown in what was locally called the "Valley of Longevity" was rich in antioxidants and the water there had a unique mineral balance. Several years later, having grown skeptical, the same author commissioned several researchers to check up on his finds, and they reported not a single centenarian in the village and that life expectancy in Vilcabamba "is in fact less than in the U.S." In the almost thirty years since then, when it's been clear that living in Vilcabamba isn't a shortcut to health or long life and is in fact more like a short circuit of both, the village has nevertheless become "one of the hottest destinations for outsiders seeking their own little piece of Shangri-La," according to one widely roaming travel writer, and "an uncanny magnet and New Age watering hole for soul-searchers."

So the cross-currents running through Ecuador are wide and deep, and even the country's champions find that they may have to unlearn what might be ingrained in their minds. One word I try to keep in my head as a quickie reminder not to draw premature conclusions is *jipijapa*, pronounced "hippy hoppa." That's the Ecuadorian name for a Panama hat, the snappy, lightweight, black-banded, handmade straw hat prized by many in the Western Hemisphere as the ultimate summer hat. But Panama hats actually come from the coast of Ecuador, where they started being woven four hundred years ago. The confusion comes from the fact that, about two hundred years later, Ecuadorians started sending them in bulk to Panama as their principal global distribution point, since from there they could easily be shipped across either the Atlantic or the Pacific. Even knowing what I knew, of course I had to buy one.

CHAPTER SEVEN

THE
HONORABLE CHAIN

THE MORNING AFTER OUR ARRIVAL IN ECUADOR, WITH
Rosa the SimMom in tow, David Gaus and I started off on the
drive to Santo. It's a long trip that Gaus, who himself lives in
Quito, personally enjoys and calls "my commute," since it's a
variant of the route he's been following for twenty years. It's an
eighty-mile drive that even now, with much better roads than existed years ago and all of them paved, takes three hours (rather
than seven, as it used to), since even on good roads much of it has
on one side of the road a precipitous, winding plunge down the
slopes of the Andes.

Gaus, who looked rested after only a few hours of sleep, was
wearing chinos and a white polo shirt with the green-and-white
AHD logo: a family of four standing in front of a tall, snow-
capped mountain. He seems to take all the time spent behind the

44

wheel in stride (in addition to the half-day drives from Quito, the two AHD hospitals are an hour and a half from each other). Back at the beginning of Gaus's Ecuador work, this Quito-to-countryside run was itself the final leg of a three thousand-mile-long commute: For an eight-year stretch, at a time when money was tight and Gaus was deliberately living on a very thin shoestring, he semiregularly reversed direction and signed up for shifts in the Milwaukee emergency room of the same hospital where he'd done his family medicine residency. It was summertime work for the most part, supplemented by periodic two-week stints during the winter. He was also a teacher during these U. S. summers, working with the hospital's new family medicine residents.

En route Gaus said:

> ER work was a cash cow. At the same time, I was getting more and more comfortable treating really sick patients, which prepared me for my work in Ecuador. Somehow all the pieces were coming together, very invigorating for a young man—chomping on an espresso, jumping on a plane. I'd go from pinching every penny in Ecuador to ordering $75,000 worth of tests in a single shift in Milwaukee. An incredibly stark contrast, separated by only 36 hours. It didn't frustrate me—I felt privileged—it was like a gift, getting to see two vastly different worlds almost simultaneously. Except that slowly they began to seem like the same single world with a lot of complexities to it. Both sides needed help. U. S. health care is the most expensive per capita in the world, but the States are only at number 37 in the World Health Organization ranking of national health systems—Ecuador's number 111, by the way, out of 190.

> But beneath the obvious difficulties are unexpected similarities, and both are inadequate when it comes to a complete picture of health. In their own ways, each country overemphasizes the doctor part of the doctor-patient relationship. The U. S. model leans too heavily on the science and technology of medicine, shortchanging the art of it. This brings us

into the realm of hermeneutics—of interpretation—a word theologians apply to Bible study but that can also refer to studying patients by paying attention to things like body language, tone of voice, and family events. In the U.S., if a middle-aged heavy smoker has a pulmonary embolus, a blood clot in his lung, he'll be started on warfarin, a blood thinner. Let's say he returns to the emergency department six months later with a second clot. The doctors there will be fascinated by his CT scan and by the pharmacology of warfarin and how its levels in the blood have to be properly monitored to prevent future clotting. But if they hear that the patient stopped taking the drug three weeks earlier and started smoking again, chances are they'll just send him home with a stern warning about no more smoking and staying on the medication.

But did anyone stop to ask why he abandoned treatment or went back to smoking? Did anyone discover he was demoted at work and that his wife was recently diagnosed with cancer? That his wife is everything to him, and the stress is unbearable? Failure to address those issues could cost him his life. You might think that on the Ecuadorian side, with so much less technology available, the art of medicine could come to the fore. That's not the case. Two public institutions, the Ministry of Public Health and the Ecuadorian Institute of Social Security—the IESS, an acronym for Instituto Ecuatoriano de Seguridad Social—provide more than 80 percent of all health care services. Short-staffed and overburdened, they have lost their ability to treat individuals and instead channel masses of humanity through a system that in too many instances is, unfortunately, dehumanizing.

The "two worlds but actually one" I've lived has helped me and Diego to a couple of core principles in our work: We strive to keep the art of medicine on par with the science and technology, which of course we stay on top of so we can know when to look beyond them. We try to instill the same thinking in our residents. It's the kind of lesson that ultimately will benefit doctors and health in any country anywhere.

This was my first sustained exposure to Gausian conversation, which often leads off in surprising directions. It was also the morning I learned that one thing David Gaus is *not* is a *camarón*, a shrimp, which is what Ecuadorians call timid drivers, alluding to them elliptically—"How much by the pound?" Gaus drives with confidence, even exuberance. On Ecuadorian roads, which are still mostly two-lane, the assumption is, he says, that "where there's room for two cars, there's room for three." Attainable speeds are uneven, though, because long-haul trucks grind slowly up and down the steep slopes, accumulating behind them long convoys of cars waiting to pass. So you often see the backs of trucks up close and their warning signs, such as an angry Daffy Duck yelling, "¡¡No me siga!!" (Don't follow me!). Personally I preferred the one in English that said, "HIT ME! I NEDD THE MONEY" [*sic*].

The first part of the drive, near the top, is through dense, mist-shrouded "cloud forests," where plants are watered by fog drip. Even there some of the most vertical mountainsides are planted with corn or roamed by scrambling cows doing their best to scamper like mountain goats. Pointing to some cows, Gaus said that hillside farmers tie themselves to trees, and sometimes their cows will slip and break a leg. "Imagine what a shock it was to me as a Midwesterner to find out you could fall off a farm."

"It's a question of degree," Gaus went on, picking up our earlier conversation and again unexpectedly weaving things together into patterns I hadn't grasped yet.

He continued:

Medical neglect is unethical, criminal, but do we always improve someone's chances by spending $2,000 on a CT scan? Certainly I wasn't the only person moving back and forth through both ends of the single world—there are plenty of

Ministry of Health officials or university people on the lecture circuit giving talks. But most of them don't get to roll up their sleeves and do clinical work treating patients at either end. Early on I was forced to assume a global perspective, but an unusual and very open one—and I've tried to look through these see-both-ways glasses ever since.

It's more than just a point of view, this perspective. Because it's on this middle ground that you can move around and try things and get more creative. Let's stop to celebrate the technology of medicine for a moment. A huge part of why modern medicine has actually improved has to do with sneaking past a great health barrier that not even microscopes can penetrate. Finally drawing back a curtain and piercing a veil as old as doctoring itself—namely, getting past our own skins. We're the beneficiaries of two hundred years of advances that tell doctors more about what's actually happening inside us, letting them look around within the living human body and listen to its inner workings without having to cut it open.

The first great breakthrough of this kind of access is curled around the shoulder of every hospital doctor, nurse, and medical technician: the stethoscope. It's not just a badge of office, like a white lab coat. Before the stethoscope was invented in France, in 1816, there was no nonlethal way of exploring internal anatomy. Learning how to listen through a stethoscope is like learning to distinguish different birdsongs. A heart murmur is just that—a turbulent flow of blood between the two regular beats. Let's say someone comes in who "looks like" he has pneumonia, a lung inflammation. He complains of chest pains, has trouble breathing, and is coughing up sputum, a yucky, gooey, yellow mixture of saliva and mucus from the lungs. You do a physical exam—you listen, prod, look, and feel. That's old-fashioned stuff, hands-on, but your hands are also advanced, sophisticated medical equipment.

You percuss, gently tapping the chest wall like a drum with a finger, and instead of hearing a hollow sound there's a kind of dullness or fullness." [Gaus took a moment to explain that medical "percussion" was introduced in the eighteenth century by an Austrian physician who as a boy had tapped the wine casks in the cellar of his father's inn to see how full they were.] Applying a stethoscope will typically show signs of "consolidation"—a region of the lungs filled with fluids—indicated by crackling or bubbling sounds, called rales, or by wheezing. Or maybe you can hear a rub, the squeaking or grating sounds that inflamed lung tissue makes when it rubs against the lining of the lung cavity. A rub sounds just like walking on freshly fallen snow. With this patient you might not even need an X-ray, a blood count, or any kind of test to confirm your diagnosis. You put him on antibiotics, and give him cough medicine and aspirin or ibuprofen to reduce his fever.

On the other hand, Gaus said as an aside, those long and long-ago commutes also helped him think through a big technology acquisition, the team's recent decision to buy a CT scanner for Hospital Hesburgh in Santo, a machine that in the States is probably the most widely used way of safely looking inside without cutting people open. There are about six thousand CT scanners in the United States, used as often as 72 million times a year, but there's only one other such unit, an early model, elsewhere in Santo. The inventor of the first machine, who won a Nobel Prize for it in 1979, worked for EMI, the British music company. It's been said that profits from Beatles records helped fund its development.
Gaus said:

A CT scanner is like putting X-rays in a spin dryer. In radiography it's the greatest thing since sliced bread because it actually *does* slice the bread, revolving around to take multiple cross-section images with every pass. These multi-slice CTs are relatively new, with 16-slice systems dating back to 2005. Today, after a decade of "slice wars" among manufacturers, sixty-four-slice scanners are the workhorses at most U.S. hospitals. They cost a million dollars new, as opposed to maybe $130,000 for a sixteen-slice CT. I know this because Al Harding, a South Bend radiologist who's on the AHD board of advisors, just spent a couple of years scouring Indiana hospitals to locate anybody looking to trade up and found someone willing to sell us a 16-slice machine for $27,000. They even offered to have a General Electric service team disassemble it and pack it, and they donated spare parts.

This was a real stroke of luck. The other CT in Santo is a four-slice, the kind that was common in the States in 1970. Essentially this let Santo jump ahead thirty-five years in technology in one swoop. A sixteen-slice CT is still a very powerful machine, part of the bread and butter of American diagnostic medicine today. So is this an extravagance? When a kid falls out of a tree and is acting funny, this is exactly what we need. Because of floods and animals, many rural Ecuadorians live in houses raised up on stilts but with no railings, and falls are all too frequent. And motor vehicle accidents are a newer and worsening problem all the time.

In the immediate aftermath of a traumatic brain injury, CT scans are highly effective in detecting any kind of problem that might be life-threatening, like bleeding within or around the brain. If you don't have a CT scanner, there's that godawful journey to the capital. A CT scan is also the test of choice for acute abdominal pain, which is a common presentation among ER patients. You can feel someone's belly and observe them, but in these situations you might not get it right by yourself. It could be appendicitis, or it could be any number of things. With a CT scan you can rule out a lot of complicated problems with 96.8 percent accuracy and pin down what's wrong. We need that technology in rural Ecuador; it's going to be revolutionary for us. Very exciting, and so helpful in terms of training young residents—they need to know what's out there and not just work by the seat of their pants. Now they can learn what's an appropriate and reasonable use of these machines.

Speaking of which . . . what is "appropriate technology" for poor people? This is a topic constantly under discussion in the medical world. Often it slides off into the idea of rationing. Take laparoscopic surgery, also called keyhole surgery, which literally means looking in through the side—it's an operation that involves inserting a thin, lighted tube into a small incision either to inspect or remove something. Some people say things like CT scans and laparoscopic surgeries are "too much tech" for the poor. But without laparoscopic surgery, it takes six to eight weeks to recover from a gallbladder operation, and there'll be a lot of pain from the scar.

Actually, I think we can resolve the question if we consider "appropriate technology" to be a phrase that's missing a word—it should be "appropriately priced technology." As nonprofit people we never stop noticing the cost of anything. For years we've kept our eyes on the MSROs—the Medical Surplus Recovery Organizations—nonprofits themselves and sort of like food banks for needy hospitals, collecting and globally distributing as much as they can of the astonishing amount of unused and still completely usable materials U.S. hospitals throw out—according to one estimate, four billion pounds' worth a year, year after year.

It could be beds, it could be an anesthesia machine, it could be sterilized needles ordered for someone's operation but left over, and simple things like needles are incredibly important. Hated as they are by patients, they're the most widely used medical device on the planet—sixteen billion injections are administered every year. Everything not rescued and packed into a forty-foot container for an overseas destination goes straight into a U.S. landfill or incinerator.

We've had mixed results with MSROs. A lot of these groups, all of them incredibly well-meaning, don't have great inventory or people who can review equipment that hospitals intend to clear out or have temporarily put into storage. The price was right, since equipment and supplies were donated and we'd only pay part of the shipping fees, but historically we could only use about a quarter of the stuff they sent us—and then we'd have to get rid of the rest of it ourselves.

About the time Hospital Hesburgh opened, we'd been just about ready to give up on MSROs, but Diego said, "I changed my mind." We'd started working with an Illinois MSRO called Mission Outreach. They were organized by a group of nuns who serve the sick, and they work closely with donor hospitals, imploring them, "Don't glean" just to have stuff to push out the door. They worked equally carefully with recipient hospitals, asking us if we knew how to maintain or even how to operate anything they might send us. We've noticed that their volunteers are meticulous in how they pack things up—only using clean, clearly labeled boxes. Some people just send big barrels of stuff, and when you unpack, there's a mishmash of catheters, tubing, all kinds of things.

I remember remarking on this to the woman who runs Mission Outreach, Georgia Winson. She said they try to make every shipment resemble, as closely as possible, an order from the original manufacturer. She was very emphatic about it, in a quiet sort of way. It has stayed with me.

Gaus quoted her as saying: "We have a 'no duct tape' rule, so there's nothing that says leftovers or feels like a hand-me-down. If we get a vinyl mattress with a tear, we'll reupholster it before sending it out. People shouldn't get dirty boxes—they are the next user in an 'honorable chain' of health and caring. Packing itself is an act of prayer. When we've filled a container we say a prayer in a circle, for the patients and the doctors and nurses."

Gaus said, "Mission Outreach handled the shipping of our CT scanner, an X-ray machine, and all sixty beds, which were donated and would've cost us $5,000 apiece. Working with Georgia's group has been a game changer—we can use 100 percent of what we get. I can't fly the residents here to Wisconsin, but I can lead them to the middle ground I discovered when bouncing between two continents. Once there you see that maybe the best term for appropriate technology would be the 'honorable chain.'"

"Just to finish off the subject," Gaus added, "please don't forget the fundamental, underlying, essential part of my ER work in the States. I wasn't looking for insight. *I needed the money.*"

CHAPTER EIGHT

LIGHTNING BOLTS

ABOUT TWO-THIRDS OF THE WAY DOWN THE STEEP ANDEAN slopes, after a quick pit stop for coffee and some excellent chocolate, the conversation took a somber turn. At first I thought Gaus was only making a casual remark, like the one he'd just made about the chocolate in Mindo, the small cloud-forest town we'd stopped at, wanting me to know that the farmers there still cultivate Nacional cacao, "heirloom" beans prized for an intense but never bitter flavor some say has a hint of black currants.

He said, in the same tone, that a few miles back we'd crossed the "snake line," an invisible, inexact, but important boundary. I waited for more, but there was a pause. After a moment Gaus said, "I was thinking about something . . . those events and conditions the ancients could only liken to lightning bolts. Lightning bolts struck me—two of them—about a week apart, just after I set up shop in Pedro. And I was helpless to do anything about it."

He offered a little background: David Warrell, a British tropical medicine specialist and WHO consultant, knighted for his exceptional work, estimates that every year over 100,000 people all over the world die from snakebites and another 400,000 are permanently maimed and disfigured.

Gaus said:

Warrell is mild-mannered and sweet-tempered, but fierce and unrelenting when he discusses snakebite. He calls it a forgotten and unfashionable disease, its victims abandoned by medical science and public health systems—among the most neglected of all neglected tropical diseases. So neglected, in fact, it wasn't until 2009 that it got added to WHO's list of "Neglected Tropical Diseases." Which calls attention to the fact that the world's poorest people aren't just suffering from HIV/AIDS, TB, and malaria, the three diseases that get the most funding. Snakebite, Warrell says, will probably stay an orphan among NTDs (neglected tropical diseases)—you'll notice how even the grimmest conditions wind up with cute acronyms all their own—because it's not infectious, you can't vaccinate people for it, and it will never be eliminated. It lacks the qualities that attract funders.

Gaus further observed:

Snakebite is specifically a danger to poor rural people—farmers and their families, including young children—because snakes live out in the countryside, and these are the same areas where health care is weakest and most underfunded. The "snake line" is my way of remembering that in Ecuador there's also a "knowledge gap" when it comes to snakes, because in Quito, where most government M.D.s who end up working in the countryside get their training, there are no poisonous snakes, which only live down here at lower altitudes. The most dangerous snake down here is a *Bothrops*—to give it its scientific name, the *Bothrops asper*—considered the ultimate pit viper. The Ecuadorians call it *equis*, the Spanish "X." [I remembered the skirts the Tsáchila men wore, criss-crossed with stripes to ward off this particular snake.] It's a large snake, up to six feet long, often found near rivers and streams. It's also an irritable and aggressive snake that has to compete for food as soon as it's born, and it can strike so fast the eye can hardly follow it. Some say that mongooses, famous for being able to attack and kill cobras, would have no better than an even chance against an *equis*.

For people the danger isn't just getting bitten—it's what happens next. Unlike a cobra bite, which is neurotoxic, paralyzing nerves and muscles, the venom in an *equis* bite, a very painful puncture, is hemotoxic, meaning it disrupts the blood system, preventing coagulation, so people can actually bleed to death. Then there's the fact that these bites don't just immobilize prey, as cobra bites do; they also seem to "pre-digest" their victims, since the venom is also a "tissue toxin" that can directly destroy the muscles around a bite—a process that seems to benefit the snake, compensating it for its oddly inefficient, underdeveloped digestive system.

The lightning bolts. . . . This was 1998. I was sitting in the small two-room storefront clinic I had just opened with a colleague in Pedro—down the street, then still unpaved, from what would later become Hospital Pedro Vicente Maldonado. "Please help my son!" I heard, from a mother whose boy, Alfredo, was seven. "The big snake bit him in the back in mid-air when he was jumping into the river to swim." It had happened only half an hour earlier, but the boy's heartbeat was erratic and he looked so bad it scared the hell out of me. Alfredo looked at me said, *"Doc, voy a morir"*—"I'm going to die." ["Doc" is the same word in English and Spanish, pronounced "Doak," with a long "o" in Spanish.]

I was startled, shocked. I'd never heard a child say that before, let alone with such resignation. I'd had some very basic training in snakebite matters in the tropical medicine department at Tulane, though it wasn't emphasized much. At the time, the general message was that snakes don't kill you. Our clinic had no anti-venom, and there was none anywhere in the area. It's an expensive medicine, about $40 a vial, and you need from four to ten vials. Children actually need more than adults. And it's the only thing that works—sucking at the wound does no good at all. Tourniquets are inefficient and if too tight can cause nerve damage. But I reassured the kid and his mom that he'd be all right, and went into emergency mode, and arranged for a truck to come pick him up and take him to Quito. He didn't even make it halfway before he died. A couple of hours later, his mom came back in absolute agony and collapsed in front of me.

It wasn't supposed to happen this way. It was gut-wrenching. Strangely, it was only then that I felt the impact of another lightning bolt, which had actually hit me the week before. A car had pulled up in front of the clinic. I smelled rotten flesh as soon as the door opened. It was Roberto, a nine-year-old boy. Gangrene had set in after an *equis* bite. It's a gruesome sight. His right leg from the knee down felt like a cold piece of dry charcoal; his foot was black, and his calf muscles were black and withered. There was no remedy except to amputate. He'd been treated by one of the private doctors in town for two weeks, with an antibiotic. Useless. After Alfredo died, we decided, for his sake and for our own, we had to become experts in snakebites. I've never seen Alfredo's mother from that day to this. I don't know if she left town or what. But I run into Roberto and his mother every so often when I'm in Pedro. He has a prosthesis on his leg and can walk without crutches.

It was time to get moving again. Before pulling out of Mindo, Gaus rummaged around in an envelope and handed me a six-page copy of an article he and Diego Herrera and two other AHD doctors had published in a medical journal in 2013—*Management of Snakebite and System Envenomation in Rural Ecuador, Using the 20-Minute Whole Blood Test*. It's a review of all 110 snakebite cases that Hospital Pedro Vicente Maldonado (HPVM) treated from 2005 to 2011. It reports, without comment, that because of the treatment methods in place, 109 patients survived—100 cases successfully handled within the hospital itself and 10 severe cases that were transferred to Quito, where one of the patients subsequently died. "There have been no further fatalities since then," Gaus said.

The article is dry and unemotional, as befits a medical journal. But having heard the backstory, I saw it as a report about successfully fulfilling a solemn pledge, creating an exemplary track record that honors a memory and rights a profound wrong. If you know what you're doing, the article makes clear, you treat a snakebite where it happened, at a nearby hospital in the Ecuadorian countryside; the doctors above the snake line are too far away and live the entirety of their lives without snakes, and they went to medical schools where the teachers didn't know much about snakes. Those doctors were trained on "the diseases of the capital." What had had to be put in place in Pedro was a first anywhere in Ecuador in terms of snakebites: proper training, procedures, tests, calmness, judgment, ongoing vigilance, and an adequate stock of supplies.

The last is a bedrock principle in this plan—always having on hand a reliable, constantly replenished supply of anti-venom. HPVM, the article notes, is "the only hospital" in the area "that regularly stocks anti-venom." Anti-venom is a late-nineteenth-century invention of one of Pasteur's protégés, Albert Calmette, a French doctor who in 1891 found himself in a village near Saigon (Vietnam was then a French colony). A flood had forced all the cobras into town, where they immediately bit forty people, killing four.

Making any kind of anti-venom is a laborious process—you have to "milk" snakes, forcing venom from their fangs. The venom is then injected into horses. The antibodies the horses produce can be safely injected into people. Once anti-venom became available, mortality fell from 25 percent of victims to less than 2 percent. Calmette's name is still so universally revered (he also developed a TB vaccine) that, according to one report, along with Pasteur's, his "is one of the few remaining French names in the Streets of Ho Chi Minh City," the former Saigon. A Brazilian doctor later came up with an anti-venom specifically effective against New World hemotoxic viper bites.

Unlike some drugs, anti-venom needs particularly careful handling. It has to be administered as soon as possible, since it's not a drug that cures—it stops any further blood or tissue damage but cannot reverse whatever damage has already been done. On the other hand, there are times it has to be avoided: Some viper bites are "dry bites" that don't inject poison, and anti-venom injections carry their own risks. They can cause fevers, rashes, and a drop in blood pressure and can induce sudden and severe allergic reactions. So this intricate and "intimidating" process (as the article calls it) is now a "required skill" taught to HPVM residents—not just the subject of a blackboard lecture heard once a year and then only vaguely remembered, because every month at least two snakebite victims will come to the hospital, more during the winter rainy season. As the article also points out, this is the only "formal medical residency program in Ecuador that provides appropriate venomous snakebite management skills."

But—and the article doesn't mention it—the quintessential test the program relies on got adopted only fairly recently. One night in Quito about twenty years ago, David Gaus, taking a chance, invited the already distinguished David Warrell, whom he had never met, out to dinner after hearing Warrell lecture on snakebites in the Amazon region, east of the Andes. Over dinner, Gaus told Warrell about the snakebite program he was putting together for the lowlands, west of the Andes. Warrell, who still vividly remembers the encounter, told Gaus that his program should of course incorporate the 20WBCT. Spelled out, the 20WBCT is the "20-minute whole-blood clotting test." Warrell is the Johnny Appleseed of the 20WBCT, a bare-bones bedside diagnostic test that, for the twenty years before his dinner with Gaus, he'd been popularizing around the world.

The 20WBCT is a blood test that lets a physician know with absolute certainty whether viper venom is present in a patient, and it's so low-tech it would barely come up in a discussion of "appropriate technology" since it practically doesn't qualify as "technology" and sounds almost too rudimentary to work. It could be called the ultimate "FBC" technique—faster, better, cheaper. It requires only a syringe, a clean test tube, and not even an elementary lab to back it up. It's fast—20 minutes—versus other tests that take a day or two for results. It's cheap, costing maybe two dollars at most, as opposed to $50 or $75 for the least sophisticated of the other tests available. There are still other tests that can cost thousands and require state-of-the-art labs.

To run a 20WBCT, all you do is draw about half a teaspoon of blood from someone bitten by a snake, let it stand in a test tube for 20 minutes at room temperature, and then tilt the test tube. Nothing more than that. If there's no venom present, the blood will have clotted, creating a kind of gooey gel and perhaps sticking to the side of the tube—meaning don't give that person anti-venom. If there is venom, the blood will still be a free-running liquid, which means you must immediately administer anti-venom. Repeat the test six hours later in every envenomed person to see if the venom has been cleared from the system. "Something simple that works," Gaus said. "That's what you love." The 20WBCT isn't universally useful—it won't show the presence or absence of cobra venom, for instance—but for a *Bothrops* bite it's infallible, and, as Herrera and Gaus's article points out, it anchors every HPVM decision about snakebite treatment.

We'd almost reached Santo Domingo. Gaus wanted to emphasize that the story of snakebite treatment is unfinished, that he's still not satisfied, that he doesn't yet feel he's done right by Alfredo. Why was that?, I wondered, considering how many people he and his colleagues have helped. "It's the anti-venom," he explained. "It's one of those incredible advances in human capacity, but it's a holdover from the early days of modern medicine." He continued:

It's still a horse serum. It's biologically active with a lot of horse antibodies mixed in, which can cause complications that bring on serum sickness, as it's called, and which typically don't show up in a patient for several days. Sure, snakebite is an underfunded and under-researched NTD. Or, better to say, NTP—a neglected tropical poison. Though acknowledging that it's neglected hasn't done much to stop it from being neglected. What's needed now is a push to produce purer anti-venoms and take horses out of the equation so we can make snakebite management less problematic, more 20WBCT-ish. I don't see that happening yet.

Our program needs to spread, but we'd like to pass along something more comprehensive. The technology exists to create new treatments that bypass horses; it's just that the companies with this capacity see little chance for profit by serving some of the poorest populations on the planet. Who will step forward? When will lightning strike again?

CHAPTER NINE

HOSPITAL
HESBURGH

THE FIRST SIGN THAT YOU'RE NEAR HOSPITAL HESBURGH, the new AHD hospital in Santo Domingo de los Colorados, is a literal one—a big billboard out on the E-20, the main highway running northwest out of Santo to the coast, just beyond the city limits. It announces to the world the "*hospital más moderno.*"

Then you have to make an abrupt, right-angle turn up a short, steep slope and follow a newly paved, narrow side street with no sidewalks for several blocks through a modest and still-under-construction residential neighborhood, one of the newer edges of this rough-and-ready town. After that you make a sharpish right turn through a gate, and you've arrived at—well, something more than just a building. Which becomes clear at the outset, since as soon as you get out of your car and stretch your legs after a long drive, you see that you're not, as expected, out in the middle of a gray parking lot, but instead standing at one end of an exuberantly flowering, carefully tended public garden that has palm trees and a profusion of brightly colored, eye-catching, and well-watered shrubs bordering tidy, terraced green lawns where families are sitting and talking quietly.

It's only then that you focus on the hospital itself—an immaculately clean, L-shaped single-story building flanking two sides of the garden, its smoothly plastered walls painted in two shades of a warm golden color.

There are two separate entrances, each more than twenty feet across and covered floor to ceiling with department-store-sized, see-through plate-glass panels surrounding sliding glass doors. The entrance to the left opens directly into the hospital itself. A green sign over this door says HOSPITALIZACIÓN, while the other entrance, on the right, leads to the waiting area for outpatient services; the sign over this door says CONSULTA EXTERNA. (At the far left is yet another glass door, this one more modestly scaled, that goes to the emergency room—and the sign over it says EMERGENCIA.) Both entrances are flanked by sturdy, gleaming white pillars sitting on square pedestals under sheltering porticos, and there are several more pillars, also white, along a covered colonnade between the entrances. Outside the main doors, the floor, an outward extension of the lobby just inside, is made of highly polished squares of brown marble kept unscuffed with repeated waxings throughout the day.

The overall effect is unusual—it's all understated, it seems to just *happen*—but there's an immediate sense of spaciousness, calm, reassurance, invitation and welcome, a reaching out to the community beyond. There's also a sense of things growing in abundance with a broad sky arching overhead. Here is a pavilion in a garden. You could be on the grounds of a children's museum or a hip art museum. The place looks brand new and at the same long-settled and as if it has put down roots there for the long haul.

This impression is all the more vivid because, inevitably, it creates such a strong contrast with the ghost image of what you're *not* seeing. When you hear "hospital," what picture comes to mind? Not to single it out particularly, but there's a big, remodeled Ministry of Public Health public hospital in Santo that I drove past a day later, which has that austere, impersonal, no-frills look I associate with hospitals; it's five stories high and seems very much set apart from the street life outside, in part, no doubt, because it's surrounded by a ten-foot-high fence of narrow steel slats. It shows the world a clean but unsmiling façade of white panels with tinted green windows, a self-contained, uneasy amalgam of office building and factory, a familiar pattern in the developed world as well. The hospital is a Correa-era construction project eager to present a contemporary look, but form and function have drifted further apart; too many modern hospitals come across as withdrawn and inward-looking, as if they were holdovers from an earlier era when, in the States and elsewhere in the developed world, most people's *camino a la cura* involved staying far away from hospitals.

After all, even in North America it was only a few generations back, as one medical review I saw pointed out, that hospitals, "with the rise of aseptic techniques, improved means of managing acute surgical diseases, and new diagnostic technologies, such as X-ray machines," finally "became a place to be cured rather than for the dying" and were no longer thought as "a last resort."

It wasn't until just before World War II that North American doctors gained confidence in their ability to cure—as Lewis Thomas, the physician, poet, and National Book Award–winning essayist, never forgot because it had all happened the year he had been an intern. Following is a slightly abridged excerpt from his 1983 book, *The Youngest Science: Notes of a Medicine-Watcher*:

For most of the infectious diseases on the wards of Boston City Hospital in 1937, there was nothing to be done beyond bed rest and good nursing care. Then came the news of sulfanilamide, and the start of the real revolution in medicine. I remember the astonishment when the first cases of pneumococcal and streptococcal septicemia were treated in Boston in

1937. The phenomenon was almost beyond belief. Here were moribund patients, who surely would have died without treatment, improving in their appearance within a matter of hours and feeling entirely well within the next day or so. For an intern, it was the opening of a whole new world. We had been raised to be ready for one kind of profession, and we sensed that the profession itself had changed at the moment of our entry. We heard about the possibility of penicillin and other antibiotics; we became convinced, overnight, that nothing lay beyond reach for the future. Medicine was off and running.

Standing right outside Hospital Hesburgh, you get a sense that, like Lewis Thomas in his day, you might be witnessing another changeover point. Here was a hospital that, by putting you at ease, had leapfrogged ahead of U. S. hospitals, having quietly learned to convey to its visitors and staff that this is what life feels like when health becomes an everyday affair, something that can be sustained and relied on. Rather than feeling like an oasis or a respite, Hospital Hesburgh felt like a harbinger. Hope without rebar. It was the opposite of the old Gertrude Stein crack about there being no "there" there in Oakland, California. This was a "there" here, another kind of there.

Diego Herrera came out to greet us. He was dressed in dark-blue hospital scrubs, with a stethoscope around his neck; he has a graying buzz cut and strong features—he might be an Ecuadorian cousin of James Gandolfini, a resemblance strengthened by the fact that the same impish grin can appear. I asked him and Gaus about the impressions I'd gotten from the hospital, and Herrera said it was entirely intentional.

Sure, he said, they were making creative use of the property, which was unusually big, eight acres in size, and they'd been able to get it for a good price. It had been a private high school that had gone out of business ten years before, and a lot of the land had never been built on to leave room for playing fields. This was why some of the plantings were so mature, and also why, since they'd saved money by remodeling the school rather than replacing it—which would've cost five to ten times as much—the hospital was just a single-story building. Former classrooms turned out to make good consulting rooms. But everything else had been very deliberately planned—and planted.

"David and I did the plantings together," he said. "We wanted to convey an atmosphere of serenity, of security. We want people to know this is an important place. We're here to help you restore yourself, and we're not going to make you anxious. Santo Domingo is all about people starting again and not stewing and getting stuck in constraining traditions, but what's missing in the town is institutionality. Everything's still very provisional and for the moment. People here need something solid and lasting."

Gaus said:

The columns were my idea. People are so used to dank, dark hospitals, I thought by putting a line of columns out front, we'd give people something to be proud of, as well as a sense of strength and permanence, something you can count on. Carondelet Palace, the Ecuadorian White House in Quito, has twenty columns on the front portico. Our columns aren't structural—just so you know, they don't hold anything up—they're cinderblock covered with spackle. I know Diego thinks I was extravagant, but they didn't cost all that much. The extra, in-between columns along the colonnade don't quite line up at the corner, but we put a tree there, and no one's noticed.

You step inside into much hustle and bustle, but the calmness persists; the spaciousness outside carries over: The old high school, built when air-conditioning was practically unheard of in rural Ecuador, used traditional tropical construction techniques for beating the heat—extra-tall ceilings and cross-ventilation. They still work, and now support the modern touches the hospital has added to the large outpatient waiting area just inside the front door. Even with a blazing sun outside, there's always a cool breeze flowing across the rows of sleek-looking and unusually comfortable metal mesh chairs. People sit there, couples and families, and keep their eyes on the list of names displayed on a large flat-screen monitor over the registration desk as they wait their turn to see a doctor, therapist, or technician—there's an electronic *bloop* once someone's name is called.

Meanwhile, a crawl across the bottom of the screen offers details about the many available services, among them family consultation, physical therapy, speech therapy, urology, *ecografía y rayos x* (ultrasound and X-rays), pediatrics, and dentistry. The pairing of physical therapy and speech therapy is unique in Santo and addresses what Herrera calls "a fairly significant need in the community, letting us chip away at that a bit." I'd wondered why a hospital was offering speech therapy, and he explained: "Many children with cerebral palsy or autism who can benefit from physical therapy are also language-challenged to one degree or another, but outside Hospital Hesburgh, the few speech therapists in the area seem scattered around town almost randomly. The combination approach helps older people, too, since after a stroke, many adults have to learn all over again how to use their tongues and lips, and in some cases how to swallow."

Beyond the lobby there's a long, wide corridor to the right, also inherited from the high school, that's an indoor breezeway with open-air windows along one wall and more than a dozen treatment rooms along the other. Outside is an old paved court that still has a couple of basketball hoops. Head left and you find on a green rug of artificial grass a little kids' playground with a brightly colored plastic slide that has round windows on the bottom to crawl through and turrets up top to clamber on. Next to it is a miniature Japanese-inspired rock garden, extending the feeling of serenity. Just around the corner is the hospital *farmacia*, and then, stretching off to the right, there's a big, high-ceilinged dining room with windows along one wall, and a new plastic roof has replaced the high school's tin roof. It's outfitted with long movable tables and lots of chairs. The full-service *cafetería* kitchen can make lunches for two hundred people a day; this in itself is a huge innovation—at many Ecuadorian hospitals, families accompanying patients have to bring their own food.

The main hospital building also has a big lobby with more sleek metal mesh seats; there's a waiting area for any imaging (CT scans, X-rays, ultrasound) that needs to be done, while all the actual *hospitalización* wards are off to the right. Even the corridors are so wide they could be rooms, easily accommodating a group of seven or more residents making rounds or two wheeled hospital beds heading in opposite directions. There are some private rooms and wards of four beds, each with its own fan—the days of giant sixteen- or twenty-bed wards are over. There's an infectious ward behind double doors that has negative air pressure—a ventilation system allows fresh air to come into each room but won't let it escape into other rooms, thus preventing cross-contamination and the spread of airborne contagious diseases such as chickenpox, measles, or the flu. A few rooms are air-conditioned—those in the intensive-care unit, the operating room, the labor and delivery rooms. The emergency room, which is open 24/7, has cubicles for up to fifteen patients.

The simulation lab sits in its own small building off to the right of the outpatient department. Then there's the "back 40"—all the extras that visitors and patients don't usually get to see, such as the *laboratorio*, the high school's old chem lab, which the school had deliberately placed in its own freestanding one-story building in case anything went wrong. Among its other features, the lab can create its own microbiology studies now that it's equipped with lab ovens for drying cultures of suspected diseases and ULT (ultra-low-temperature) freezers for preserving these cultures at temperatures as low as eighty degrees below zero Celsius, along with carefully enclosed benches that create aseptic work areas and have hoods that let in only filtered air, making it possible to (safely) test for microbacteria that can poison food or contaminate water.

Behind the main hospital there's a dorm for residents (two beds per room); at the back corner of the hospital is the *cuarto de limpieza*, a cleaning—literally, the cleanliness—room, which looks like a gas station for cleaning supplies, with colored tubes leading off from big jugs dispensing different products. Nearby is the laundry room, with enormous washing and ironing machines— "This is one of the things that really makes a difference day to day," Herrera said on a back-of-the-house tour—"considering that the traditional alternative was always a team of older ladies using tubs. The first washing machine we bought was for the hospital in Pedro when it opened—it's a UniMac, a monster, renowned for ruggedness and reliability. We're still using it there. It hasn't needed maintenance once in fifteen years."

In the un-built open space all around are leftover volleyball courts, a netless tennis court, a soccer field, and a half-mile-long path around the edge of the property that residents use as a running track. Then there are all the trees the high school planted: banana trees, passionfruit trees, and so-called "tree tomatoes," whose semisweet, egg-shaped fruit gets blended with peppers, onions, and lime juice to make *aji*, the hot sauce that sits on every Ecuadorian table and is said to date from the time of the Incas.

"We could build a medical school back there," Gaus said in the room he uses upstairs from the sim lab. "Or a university, if we have to." Maybe they won't have to, because maybe they've already done it, in a new way that might be called laparoscopic— low-risk and minimally invasive, making a small and almost invisible hole in the side of something rather than attacking a problem massively from the front.

During my next few days at Hospital Hesburgh, as I heard more about the situations and conditions it has to handle, this still-unfinished project brought to mind a much older building that gives off a different kind of radiance, the Iglesia de la Compañía de Jesús, probably the most glorious structure in Quito, an enormous Jesuit church that took 160 years to build, starting in 1605. At one point a couple of hundred years later, it was so neglected that a forest had begun growing through the floor. Now restored, its interior glows continuously because both daylight and candlelight reflect off a hundred pounds of floor-to-ceiling gold leaf. You could say that the defining purpose of the Compañía is to intensify the connections people feel to the world to come, while Hospital Hesburgh strengthens their ties to the world we already live in. The Compañía blends and balances markedly different and, in other hands, clashing and incompatible styles of architecture, ranging from those of the Arab Middle East to the Incan and to several centuries' worth of European baroque and neoclassical. The confluence at Hospital Hesburgh is a reconciliation of two very different approaches to global health, the arcs of two storylines. More than being an end point, it also launches a new story.

The canton of Pedro Vicente Maldonado has a population of ten thousand, composed primarily of farmers and ranchers and their families.

The lush landscape of Pedro Vicente Maldonado in Ecuador's northwest lowlands.

All photos courtesy of Andean Health and Development.

Andean Health and Development's first home, a storefront clinic (1997).

Hospital Pedro Vicente Maldonado (left) and its surrounding rural community.

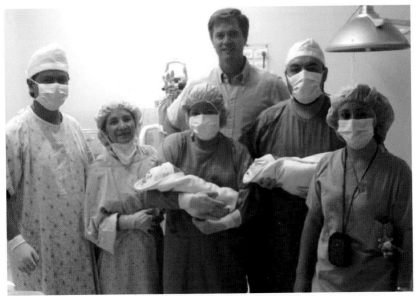

Dr. David Gaus joins the first Family Physician resident trainees in the labor and delivery suite of Hospital Pedro Vicente Maldonado.

Family physicians in Andean Health and Development's three-year residency program.

Hesburgh Hospital, Santo Domingo de los Colorados, Ecuador.

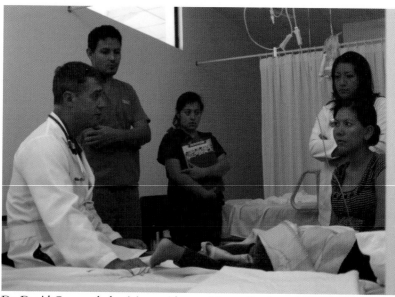

Dr. David Gaus and physician residents with a pediatric patient and her mother.

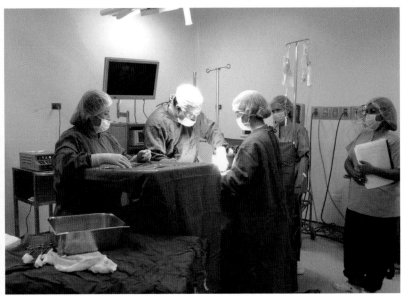

Hesburgh Hospital's operating room.

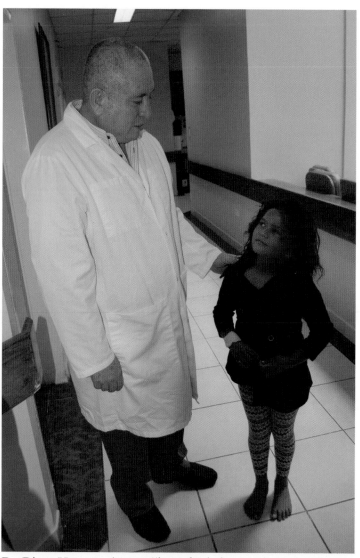

Dr. Diego Herrera, vice president of Saludesa, with a young patient who survived a traumatic motorcycle accident.

Rev. Theodore M. Hesburgh (1917–2015), co-founder and board chair of Andean Health and Development and president of the University of Notre Dame (1952–1987).

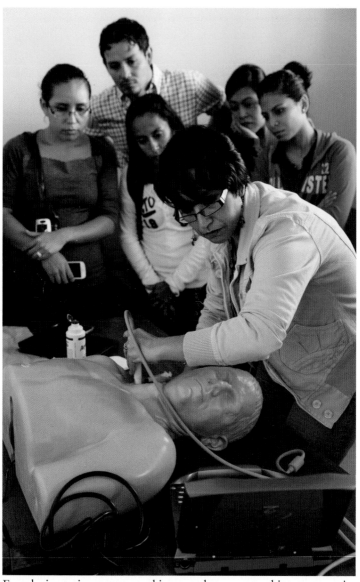

Ecuadorian trainees engrossed in procedure on a teaching mannequin.

CHAPTER TEN

WHERE'S COCO?

THERE'S AN EXTRAORDINARY VARIETY OF PROBLEMS
coming in the front door at Hospital Hesburgh, a far greater
range than U.S. hospitals encounter. On my first day there, the
place had its hands full, though there had been only three new admissions that morning (an unusually small number). One of the
patients was a middle-aged diabetic man whose new diabetes
management program was too aggressive and, as a result, he had
begun to develop kidney problems. This man had come from the
outer edge of the hospital's catchment area; he'd caught a forty-
five-minute ride on an early morning milk truck making a run
on a rural road, which brought him to another road closer to
town, where he got on a bus that after another forty-five minutes
brought him to the hospital.

The second patient, a young man also from the countryside, had sliced his thumb working on a machine that cuts balsa

wood and has a guillotine-like blade. Ironically, he was a casualty of sustainability. Ecuador has 95 percent of the world's production of balsa, though the tree is found from Guatemala to Bolivia. This fast-growing, so-called "featherweight" wood, which has a lighter density than cork, is well known to generations of model-airplane builders, but is now raised in dense plantations and shipped to the United States in bales for use on wind farms as part of the sandwich of materials in wind-turbine blades, some over two hundred feet long, the wingspan of an Airbus.

The third patient was a 30-year-old woman with huge, swollen lymph nodes who, a week before, had gone to a hospital in Quito, where she was told she had an abscess in her neck that needed draining. When this was done, she was discharged. By the time she reached Hospital Hesburgh, she was so weak she couldn't walk and in so much pain that, as one of the doctors said, "Her hair was hurting." She was given prednisone, a steroid, to reduce the swelling. By that evening, according to the same doctor, she "was feeling like Aphrodite." Her problem had not been a neck infection. What she'd come down with—what the Quito hospital had missed—was chikungunya, a mosquito-transmitted viral infection originally from East Africa that causes fever and severe joint pain that can persist for months or even years.

Chikungunya virus, or CHIKV, became epidemic in Ecuador several years ago, with hundreds of cases in Santo and Pedro, even before the arrival of the Zika virus, also mosquito-transmitted and also originally from East Africa. There is no vaccine against or cure for either virus at this point—nor, for that matter, is there any cure for dengue fever, still another virus prevalent in Ecuador and carried by mosquitos that originated far from the Americas— again, probably in Africa, but perhaps in China. Also known as breakbone fever, dengue produces a high fever, joint and bone pain, and a characteristic rash.

Perhaps not every hospital, even if it had gotten the diagnosis right, would have been overly concerned about the woman admitted to Hospital Hesburgh with chikungunya: Her case came near the tail end of an epidemic outbreak. It seems to be one of those diseases that "burns its way" through a population and then fades rather that settling in for a sustained period, as dengue has. No one is predicting, yet, what course Zika will take in Ecuador—it recently appeared in Quinindé, a town of 30,000 people about an hour's drive from Santo toward the Pacific coast.

But AHD doctors are keeping a vigilant watch on all three viruses—dengue, CHIKV, and Zika—as potentially highly dangerous public-health threats over the long run and as warning signs of things to come. Zika is the only one currently ascendant and the one people all over the world have already heard of, generating frightening headlines after it was demonstrated that, though most people who contract it never even know they've had it, the virus is devastating to some pregnant women; it can lead to profound and irreversible birth defects, among them microcephaly, an abnormality characterized by a small head caused by the brain's not having developed properly in the womb. One recent estimate says Zika could spread through the Americas for about three years and infect more than 93 million people, including one and a half million women of childbearing age; it might then explode again ten years after that.

What alarms AHD doctors about CHIKV is the disease and how you get it. CHIKV is seldom benign. It can cause severe arthritis, encephalitis (brain inflammation), fluid buildup around the heart, and Guillain-Barré syndrome, a temporary weakening and even paralysis of the legs and arms, something that's also been associated with Zika. All these complications have been seen at Hospital Hesburgh and at HPVM. "Chikungunya won't kill you," one of the AHD doctors told me, "but it can make you want to die."

Even more worrisome are the "vectors," the mosquitos involved (a vector carries a disease but doesn't cause it). There are 3,549 species of mosquitos on the planet, fewer than two hundred of which bite humans. Those that do have different habits and preferences—the *Anopheles* mosquitos that transmit malaria, for instance—do most of their biting between nine at night and five in the morning, so sleeping under a mosquito net offers protection. Not so with *Aedes aegypti*, the mosquito that can transmit CHIKV, Zika, and dengue, all three; in this context they're considered the "unholy trinity" of viruses. *A. aegypti*, which arrived in South America from Africa long before CHIKV, probably as a passenger on slave ships, can bite at any time, day or night.

Then there is the parallel presence of a newer arrival, *A. albopictus*, the Asian tiger mosquito, which gets its name from its elegantly white-striped legs and body; it's an aggressive all-day biter that prefers the countryside and biting outdoors, and it can tolerate cooler temperatures than *A. aegypti*. Long known to transmit dengue fever and a couple of dozen other viruses, though historically not associated with chikungunya, the Asian tiger mosquito, aka the forest mosquito, has been singled out as "one of the fastest-spreading animal species" and as "currently the most invasive mosquito species in the world," according to *Spread of the Tiger*, a definitive 2008 public-health review. Most likely, it got to the Western Hemisphere in the 1980s from Southeast Asia.

This mosquito seems to have arrived in North America as an unseen accompaniment to the importation of so-called "lucky bamboo" houseplants, which grow in water, are extremely easy to maintain, and are protected by an ancient Chinese tradition that says they bring prosperity and happiness. The mosquito probably reached South America in far bigger numbers in container ships at much the same time, after a huge global market in tires from used cars, trucks, and planes opened up as a result of heightened safety concerns. Under then-new vehicle regulations, countries like Japan categorized old tires with worn treads as unsafe. Instead of being scrapped, these tires were sold to dealers in the United States, who then resold them to countries in Latin America. It was a kind of "inappropriate technology" transfer.

Unnoticed by anyone at the time, the mosquitos, which in their home countries were a nonmigratory species that would travel less than half a mile in a lifetime, hitched a ride to the New World by laying their eggs in the truck tires. The story gets more complicated still, beginning even before the mosquitos had access to the tires. After World War II, deforestation programs cleared land for farmers, roads, and other development. This pushed various mosquito species, including the forest mosquito, out of the woods in which they had evolved ages before, into active, sustained, and seemingly permanent human contact. Perhaps the mosquitos had long been hosts to viruses that had previously been confined to forests. This phenomenon, the spread to humans, is known as "spillover."

So CHIKV and Zika epidemics can be explained by looking at two successive timelines—continent-jumping mosquitos become established in new locations and are thus already in place and available to be used by continent-jumping diseases when, at some later time, a few infected people show up.

A case in point: According to one estimate, Zika probably reached the Americas from Southeast Asia "in a single traveler" who came to Brazil on a plane sometime during the second half of 2013, perhaps to attend a run-up game to the World Cup. (Commercial airlines now carry three billion passengers around the world every year, one reason why viral outbreaks have more than tripled since 1980.) The two timelines converged once the disease reached Brazil. Because of a prolonged drought in the country, people had begun storing water in their homes, creating indoor breeding grounds for the mosquitos already present.

But the extra dimension of why AHD doctors have been keeping such a close watch on CHIKV—"a very interesting virus," as both a U.S. expert and the AHD doctors using neutral language will say—is that this virus, most unusually, has become an opportunistic leaper across yet another kind of physical barrier previously thought of as insuperable. It can jump vectors. It has now been demonstrated that CHIKV, through a seemingly insignificant mutation involving a single amino acid, can actually switch hosts, and in that way infest both *A. aegypti* and the closely related but even more wide-ranging Asian tiger mosquito while maintaining the same level of virulence in both species. It's a "clear switch," as an online 2015 article in *Nature Medicine* put it. "In theory, such an adaptable virus could travel worldwide. It nearly has."

Things were a lot simpler a hundred years ago when, at the dawn of epidemiology and biomedicine, Dr. Walter Reed, the celebrated U. S. Army surgeon, demonstrated that it was bites from *A. aegypti* that transmitted yellow fever—not, as had been supposed, direct contact with an infected person. This discovery led to anti-mosquito programs in Central America and allowed for the resumption of work on the Panama Canal, a project the French construction company that successfully built the Suez Canal had abandoned in bankruptcy, scandal, and despair after tens of thousands of workers had died from yellow fever.

It perhaps also demonstrates that in the presence of global warming, maybe there's no such thing as tropical medicine anymore—only universal medicine, or something close to it. Larger animals like tropical snakes, such as the *Bothrops*, aren't likely to leave their original surroundings and may only gradually increase their range as temperatures warm, but, on the other hand, by 2016 the Asian tiger mosquito was already established as far north as Vermont and was about to reach Wisconsin, David Gaus's home state. That's 1,500 miles north of the tropics.

This means that we're entering an era in which medical personnel in tropical and semitropical areas often encounter emerging and soon-to-be-widespread diseases first. So doctors at facilities like Hospital Hesburgh are no longer toiling in isolated outposts but have become the first responders in a public-health phenomenon that, more and more, envelops both the developed world and the developing world. World Health Organization researchers are already speculating what virus will go global next. One candidate is the Nipah virus (NiV), a virus that can cause brain inflammation, which was originally confined to fruit bats and pigs in Malaysia and India.

Now that diseases won't stay localized and the places where they show up are more like way stations than destinations, doctors in warm regions have a new role as sounders of the alert. In 2015 Zika got taken very seriously very quickly, in a matter of months, in that case perhaps inevitably so, since birth defects were seen in Brazil less than a year before athletes from all over the world would be coming to Rio de Janeiro for the Summer Olympics.

CHIKV, an infection with serious consequences of its own—and one that has demonstrated it can double its threat by leaping from one species of mosquito to another—may never get the same intensity of attention. But since notoriety is no substitute for thoroughness, each CHIKV case that comes before the doctors at Hospital Hesburgh and HPVM is carefully tracked and information about it compiled into a database on behalf of the rest of us, a group that could soon include both North and South Americans.

These doctors are better equipped to make sense of this information than any other group in rural Ecuador, because they're the first paperless hospitals in the Ecuadorian countryside—all their records are electronic, keyed into a central EMR (electronic medical record) system through iPads and laptops. Every doctor and every resident at both hospitals has a tablet or laptop. Hospital information is accessible and displayable on these laptops and on flat-screen TVs; routers are embedded in the ceilings. The software to support such a program for rural hospitals didn't exist in Spanish, so Gaus and Herrera found a programmer at a college in Santo to build a program they could use. Now it handles notes on current cases, notes previously taken on the same patients' earlier cases, prescriptions, tests and their results, X-rays taken, procedures decided on, and how they turned out, producing a complete EHR (electronic health record) that's instantly available. Paperless hospitals have existed for only a decade, and even in the States, where they're now widespread, they were largely considered a myth, like the paperless office, as recently as 2009. Only about half a dozen other hospitals anywhere in Ecuador have gone paperless.

So far, money doesn't flow as fast as diseases spread. Despite the tablets in doctors' backpacks, it can still feel like "the back of beyond" in Santo and other rural communities in terms of having resources on hand that could be devoted to treatment or research. But there's no longer such a disconnect in terms of the problems that need to be faced or the ability of the doctors in Santo to be on top of things.

When I spoke to Gaus about this, he said going paperless was "a big deal for us"—and that the detailed patient histories "at our fingertips" could serve as a reliable extra layer of data in terms of predicting new infectious diseases likely to emerge in the Ecuadorian countryside. He described the implications of viral mutation, which were indeed scary. "In its early years," he said, "tropical medicine was fascinated by—maybe fixed on—parasites as disease agents. Parasites and worms, and then bacteria."

Some background: The first big breakthrough in the field was the late nineteenth-century demonstration by Sir Ronald Ross and Sir Patrick Manson—the "Father of Tropical Medicine"—that malaria is caused by a tiny, one-celled parasite in the red blood cells that uses a mosquito as its agent. As Gaus told me:

Before Ross and Manson, so little was known about where the disease came from. I remember when I was in med school at Tulane, in New Orleans, being shown the spot where once upon a time they used to fire cannons down the length of Canal Street, in the hopes that the vibrations might shake malaria out of the air. But in the century since Ross and Manson, we haven't had much in our arsenal to combat viruses. Maybe that's why we've tended to ignore them, despite the fact that the Spanish flu epidemic in 1918 and 1919 killed two or three times as many people as had just been killed in the First World War.

Yet nowadays viruses are the newest, biggest threat. Because some viruses can modify themselves and spread into new mosquitos, people could be reinfected with variants of the same disease. We don't know this yet—but it's possible. At the moment, once you've recovered from a bout of dengue or CHIKV or Zika, you're immune and can't get it again. So far, that's been the best piece of good news we can offer people. But it's not just that we need better diagnoses for all three, and vaccines and treatments. We have to get into the habit of expecting we're only at the beginning of the phenomenon of arboviruses—the technical name, by the way, for all arthropod- or insect-borne viruses. With the database we already have, we're collaborating with the University of Wisconsin's Global Health Institute on exactly who's coming down with what and getting bitten by what. We'll set out mosquito traps around the homes of any patient with a confirmed arbovirus case. It wouldn't shock me if we find that things have already accelerated, and our trapped mosquitos are harboring ten new viruses—displaced, casual arrivals from elsewhere in the world that no one in Ecuador has ever seen before. Reality isn't just what we've encountered so far. It's what we're likely to find and have to think about as soon as we look a little more closely.

Gaus also wanted to talk about another equally compelling pattern he'd seen in all three of that day's Hospital Hesburgh admissions once you considered them as a group. That was a topic, he said, best discussed over dinner, since it deserved a proper explanation. He grabbed Dr. Carlos Troya, head of the postgraduate residency program—and, as director of the sim lab, custodian of Rosa the SimMom. We piled in a car and drove—rapidly, of course—through a maze of streets, at one point passing another Hospital Hesburgh billboard. We headed to Gaus's favorite Santo hangout, Pescados Dónde Coco, which literally means the Where's Coco? Seafood Restaurant, though more colloquially it's a way of saying Coco's Place. It turned out to be one of the most cheerful and relaxed restaurants I've ever been to. And about the simplest.

Dónde Coco, continuously bustling and overflowing with large families from 6:30 at night until 11:00 (and virtually tourist-free), is the perfect exemplification of what Diego Herrera means when he says Santo is a hopeful and not a hidebound city. As a structure, it's basically nothing more than a brightly lighted cube of air, in some ways a virtual restaurant. Yet it works. It's a large, high-ceilinged, tin-roofed shed of a building with a lot of fluorescent lights fastened overhead that sits on a street corner, so that two sides can be completely open air and spill out onto the sidewalks under overhanging canopies. On a warm, sticky night, common for Santo, even a hint of a breeze can pass through the entire restaurant unhindered. Simple, oblong wood tables in great numbers fill most of the floor, each surrounded by lightweight, stackable plastic chairs. On one wall there's a colorful mural of fishermen's rowboats drawn up on an unnamed beach; on the back wall is a big flatscreen TV that's usually showing a soccer match; and near the check-out counter a big fish tank aswirl with giant lazing carp that exerts an irresistible pull on a succession of little kids who've wandered away from their families' tables.

The menu gives you a choice: For $3.50 you can have a freshly caught, crisply fried, medium-sized *cabezudo,* whose name is taken from a carnival figure with an oversized head. It's a low-fat, tender, remarkably sweet-tasting and big-headed Pacific Ocean fish very popular in Santo. It eats shrimp and crabs, which could explain the sweetness. Or you can order a larger *cabezudo* for $5.00. Both plates come with tomato, lettuce, onion, a wedge of lime, white rice, and fried, sliced plantains. For drinks there's orange juice and bottles of water or soda or beer. You can't go wrong. As one review on the Dónde Coco Facebook page puts it: "*Recomendado 100%.*"

By the way, where *was* Coco? Not there that night. It's the nickname of the owner, Walter "Coco"—that is, "Coconut"—Valencia. He was out of town.

CHAPTER ELEVEN

TRANSITIONS

THE THREE OF US GRABBED A TABLE NEAR THE BACK AND ordered large *cabezudos* and some beer. Gaus turned to Carlos Troya and asked him if he'd seen a pattern in that day's hospital admissions. Troya, one of AHD's breakout stars, said the question was an easy one to answer.

In 2008, in his thirties, Troya had been part of the first class of family medicine residents Gaus and Herrera had trained at HPVM the year it became a teaching hospital, and Troya was instantly hired as soon as he completed the program three years later. He had grown up in an oil-boom town in the Ecuadorian Amazon and gone to college in Quito. His favorite quote, according to his Facebook page, is from Rimbaud: "We must be absolutely modern." He has thick, dark hair and a ready smile. He was smiling now.

"*La transición epidemiológica*," Troya said. "The epidemiological transition."

I was puzzled.

Gaus jumped in: "Epidemiologists are sometimes called 'disease detectives' because they study the health problems of broad groups of people. They're an essential part of the science underpinning public heath. The 'epidemiological transition' is a phrase that became part of medicine in 1971, when Dr. Abdel Omran—an epidemiologist at the University of North Carolina, Chapel Hill—pointed out that as U.S. citizens lived longer, and as treatments improved, they were outliving the accidents and the infections, like diarrhea in infants, or pneumonia or TB, that'd previously proved lethal." He noted that life expectancy in the States for men had increased by 50 percent since 1900—from 46 to 67—and has since gone up to 76. "Instead, more and more people were succumbing to the 'noninfectious diseases,' as we call them, that tend to appear later in life. Meaning all those chronic, degenerative, noncommunicable, controllable but not curable conditions that can afflict a person, usually only as they age, like heart attacks, stroke, cancer, or diabetes—diseases that don't go away but can be managed."

Troya nodded, then picked up the thread:

Omran had an elegant way of expressing things and took the long view. He looked back through time and saw three stages to the epidemiological transition. In the first, the Age of Pestilence and Famine, when most people who survived infancy only lived to between 20 and 40, the causes of death were wars, famines, and epidemics. This is close to the biblical idea of the Four Horsemen of the Apocalypse, who appear at the end of days bringing war, famine, pestilence, and death—though Omran transposes this back to early in the human story. Then came the Age of Receding Pandemics, which he attributed to twentieth-century advances in health care, and during which people could expect to live to between 30 and

50. Finally, and following closely, was and is the Age of Degenerative and Man-Made Diseases.

"Well, yes, that's us," said Gaus, before he continued:

We're everything at once—a triple threat. Look at today's admissions. Two of them are age-old afflictions that have taken new forms. Trauma, for one. An accident out in a field with a machete is replaced by an accident on a balsa-cutting machine—though we still get machete wounds, too. Also lower back pain from bending over with a machete to cut grass for the cow. There are more road deaths—all this highway construction means more people are driving, and driving faster. It's the mortality and morbidity of modernity. Today's second case: Instead of someone with malaria from a mosquito bite, we have a woman with chikungunya from a mosquito bite—though we still see malaria cases, as well. And pneumonia cases and all the infectious diseases you can pick up from the water and the air, not just from mosquitos.

Ecuadorian life expectancy is 77 now, a little better even than the countries around us. Half a century ago it was 53. So now we have to think about health span as well as life span. We see more diabetics—like our third case today. People aren't just living longer, but getting overweight and inactive as they get older. Then there are those with other chronic, noninfectious conditions. None of that is helped by a "nutrition transition" and a "socioeconomic transition" going on at the same time. Now it's cheaper here to buy a bag of Cheetos in aluminum foil than a bunch of bananas. Which is kind of pathetic. Diets are out the window.

In the U.S., diabetes rates have finally started going down after they exploded a quarter of a century ago, with evidence that *norteamericanos* are drinking less soda and getting more exercise. There's not much a hospital in Santo can do about that. What we need to do is make sure our doctors can handle, and expect that they will be handling, anything and everything. Because the prevalence of anything and everything will be the ongoing situation here in rural Ecuador for this generation and beyond.

The *cabezudos* were long gone. We ordered another round of beer. Troya said the classic list of epidemiological transitions was in fact incomplete. From all indications, except for accidents, ancient hunter-gatherers enjoyed pretty good health, though there are suggestions from DNA research that after close encounters with Neanderthals in Europe fifty thousand years ago, the descendants of these unions became taller and less prone to schizophrenia. Researchers in Australia offer a theory that once early humans could control fire, and groups gathered around campfires, this "created the ideal conditions for the emergence of TB as a transmissible disease." Could there otherwise have been something like a primordial Age of Health among these remote ancestors? Possibly.

The first true health transition—for the worse, and the one that would correspond to Omran's Age of Pestilence and Famine—came just after the end of the last Ice Age, about ten thousand years ago. It was part of the great shift, the beginning of civilization, when hunters and gatherers in the Near East, along with others around the same time in Europe, India, and China, learned how to farm and herd so they could produce their own food. From then on they lived most of their lives in a single place instead of wandering the face of the earth, and wound up in dwellings that were right next door to their most precious new asset, the flocks of animals they had domesticated.

Life in settlements created an age that successfully conquered famine, much of the time at least, but in so doing was overwhelmed by pestilence. Looking back, it was at this point in our history that a number of infectious-disease viruses changed hosts, from the formerly wild animals to us. Smallpox and measles were originally cattle diseases. We came down with the flu from pigs and caught the common cold from horses and camels. As one medical historian has said, we'd exchanged a world where the principal danger came from macro-parasites, meaning large predatory animals, for one dominated by invisible micro-parasites.

Life expectancy, which was about 30 when the Roman Empire was at its height, stayed low throughout the Middle Ages, both before and after the Black Death—a bacterial, not a viral, infection that swept across Europe in 1348, killing between one-third and two-thirds of the continent's population. Fatal epidemics eventually dwindle once any large group of people adapts to their presence, but only those people who've been exposed acquire immunity. Thousands of years after the invention of farming, these devastating epidemics reached the Americas, where, as part of the "Columbian Exchange," they spread with Spanish explorers and invaders and had a catastrophic effect.

The second health transition came late, Gaus said, probably not until the nineteenth century if you accept the McKeown Hypothesis, the idea that industrialization—the force that transformed Europe and North America into the developed world, even if it imposed drab and dismal working conditions—improved the underlying health and lengthened the lives of factory workers by housing, feeding, and clothing them better than they had been on farms and in villages. This came before Omran's Age of Receding Pandemics, more closely related to what was essentially a third transition, the discovery of germs and how to cure infectious diseases—the change that altered the function of doctors so they weren't just caring for and looking after sick people (or, as another medical historian put it, giving the impression of caring) and had a chance to actually cure them.

From this wider perspective, the epidemiological transition of the moment, Omran's Age of Degenerative and Man-Made Diseases, is actually the fourth transition—and maybe the universalization of tropical medicine could be considered a *fifth* transition.

"So here in Santo," Gaus went on, "we're trying to lay the groundwork for an Age of Health. The 'Columbian Exchange' can still be felt here, coloring people's attitudes, and the prosperity brought by industrialization and modernization barely registers out in the countryside. As physicians devoted to rural health care, we have to be alert to *all* the transitions humanity has seen so far."

It was time to get back to the hospital. In the car, we talked about other kinds of hospitals in rural Ecuador and how they differ from the unique AHD model of smallish, self-sufficient, nonprofit facilities that reach out to the communities that surround them. It's not that there are none, Troya said—one recent count showed ninety-one small Ministry of Public Health hospitals in various parts of the countryside. But, as in other developing countries, there were really only a few alternatives that had taken root—the public hospitals, by far the most numerous group, which included a smaller number in a separate system built by the Ecuadorian Social Security Administration, or IESS (the Instituto Ecuatoriano de Seguridad Social); so-called "missionary" hospitals created by groups from other countries, most of them faith-based; and private, for-profit clinics owned by Ecuadorian doctors.

Each of these types of hospital had and has a built-in set of problems that hold things back, especially the public hospitals, shunned for generations, which still face severe challenges in terms of morale and organization, in finding and keeping fully trained personnel, and in having proper equipment and supplies— even as they've struggled, especially under Correa, to improve services and shed their old reputation by putting up ambitious structures like the hospital I saw in downtown Santo. Troya spoke highly of the quality of care—"clearly from the industrialized world"—in missionary hospitals. The weakness there is that they're entirely dependent on funding from abroad for personnel and supplies, and if the backing is withdrawn, as sometimes happens, the project ends and they drop out of the picture. The for-profit private hospitals, usually run by local M.D.s with no post-graduate training, serve only patients who can pay—maybe a third of the population in the country at large, and a much smaller percentage in rural areas.

These problems make Hospital Hesburgh and HPVM anomalies in a rural system that otherwise consists only of hospitals that welcome all but may not be able to help all; hospitals that can help everyone but may not always be there; or hospitals that only people of means can afford.

CHAPTER TWELVE

SOUVENIR

BACK AT THE HOSPITAL—I WAS USING A RESIDENT'S bedroom, temporarily empty—I listened to rumbles of thunder outside the window, which looked out on a two hundred-foot-wide green corridor on one side of the hospital grounds that covered a buried crude-oil pipeline running from oil wells east of the Andes all the way to the coast. It was hard not to think of the hospital as a pumping station along another corridor, extending its reach across the countryside. But as a nighttime storm rolled toward the city, something nagged at me.

What's being accomplished at Hospital Hesburgh, and on a smaller scale at Hospital Pedro Vicente Maldonado—that is, addressing the reality of the situation on the ground in these places—has not yet affected the most widely held assumptions in the global health community about what ought to be happening in such places. Practice, even practice that's proving itself, sharply differs from accepted theory. If I were to propose a similar program to any number of distinguished doctors and dedicated health workers around the globe, probably I'd be politely counseled to think again and come up with a better idea.

It's a situation in which to do well—meaning to do right by people, and be acknowledged as having done so—you have to be consistently better at doing good, as you've defined it, than some of the best and most sincere do-gooders in the field, the group of so-called primary health care providers. They are, and for many years have been, impatient with hospitals. They consider them a distraction and a diversion of resources away from providing proper care for poor populations, a "money suck," to use Gaus's own phrase.

This is only one side of a long-running debate, but it's been the dominant position for decades, remaining unchanged, for instance, across the span of Gaus's career—and he himself was somewhat anti-hospital when he came back to Ecuador in 1997. It was only then that he discovered, with his team, that in order to be of real service, he had to build first one and then a second rural hospital; subsequently realized he had to find novel ways of paying for both that didn't increase the cost of care; and after that saw that these small, rural, nonprofit hospitals could be launching pads if they became teaching institutions capable of working beyond their own walls, creating a constantly renewed series of trained young doctors ready to invigorate and strengthen the work of other rural hospitals.

"Primary health care"—it's a technical term, but not a satisfying one. On the one hand, primary care refers to the people you turn to first when you get sick—for example, your own "primary care physician." (In Ecuador, these doctors are called "first-level" physicians.) But "primary" is also part of an academic classification system used to identify who handles what, based on schooling and degrees received, that parallels the idea of primary schools, secondary education, etc. Except that this model is a pyramid, the base of which is public health services (clean water campaigns, "health promotion" programs that tell people how to take better care of themselves, and so on). Primary care in this context is one level "above" such instruction and information, and refers to a general practitioner or an outpatient clinic. "Secondary care" refers to a general hospital (like HPVM or Hospital Hesburgh), while a "tertiary care hospital" will have specialists on staff with advanced training, such as heart surgeons or neurosurgeons; when most North Americans say "hospital," this is the kind of place they probably have in mind.

From the patient's point of view, though, the object is to *avoid* graduating from one level to another: Keeping your blood pressure under control can prevent a heart attack that will require acute hospital care. This doesn't always work out—spend a few days in an emergency department, Gaus says, dealing with strokes, childbirth complications, car crashes, and the like, and you'll see how many people's introduction to medical care is at the tertiary level.

As used here, "primary health care" means anything done for people before they go to a hospital. The ongoing question is this: What are the most effective ways to help as many people as possible in developing countries, which in the past had only rudimentary systems or, in the case of former colonies, where people felt condescended to in hospitals staffed by European doctors who, it was suspected, were only interested in creating outposts far from home where "white people wouldn't die."

How do you get beyond this? Would you train a new elite or instead mobilize communities to take matters into their own hands? If you could prevent people from getting sick in the first place, wouldn't that be more effective and cheaper than curing them after they were already ill?

I had with me a present for Gaus and his team—an unusual souvenir of this century-long dispute whose origins, unlikely as it sounds, stretch back to the trenches dug in France for the First World War.

In 1916—this is perhaps one of the least reported features of World War I, though something that made it truly worldwide—the French and British recruited 140,000 farm workers, then called "coolies," from eastern China to work in factories, build roads, and dig trenches along the Western Front. Some, it's been said, were from villages so isolated that when they were assembled in Shanghai and saw the eight- and ten-story buildings lining the Bund, they were convinced they had already reached Europe. Their story is still so unknown they've been called "the forgotten of the forgotten."

Their presence in France changed the life of Jimmy Yen, more formally known as Y. C. James Yen. Yen was born in Sichuan and was sent on a scholarship to Yale. He'd just graduated in 1918 when the YMCA sent him to France as an interpreter and supervisor for the Chinese laborers. He was assigned to a camp of five thousand men digging trenches. At night they asked him to write letters home, but the volume of requests soon became overwhelming. So he started to teach literacy, and "for the first time in my ignorant intellectual life," he wrote, realized that illiterate villagers, whom he had been told were unteachable and incapable of learning, had been denied "not brains, for God has given that to them, but opportunity."

Working with a group of forty men, Yen, a charismatic man with, as friends said, a "forceful personality," came up with a simplified set of written Chinese characters (a thousand, pared down from the eight thousand he'd learned in school). The forty men then taught others, and soon the five men in his camp were learning to read and write—which so impressed a British major that he sent Yen to all the other Chinese camps at the front. The result was that, by the end of the war, most of the 140,000 were literate. Yen called this "the release of the pent-up, God-given powers in the people," saying, "We do not offer relief to the poor, but release."

The Jimmy Yen story was just beginning. Again in China, after the war, he organized the Mass Education Movement, which, over the next fifteen years, brought literacy to sixty million people. In 1926, through the creation of the Ding Xian Experiment, off in a rural county of 400,000 in the flat Chinese countryside a hundred miles southwest of Beijing, Yen decided to tackle more ambitious goals after a village elder told him (according to

Yen's biographer), "Dr. Yen, I am grateful to know how to read, but my stomach is just as empty as my illiterate neighbor's."

While continuing the literacy campaign, the challenge was to develop new kinds of tools—simple and low-cost, analogous to the simplified Chinese characters Yen had devised in France, which entire communities could use to remedy "weaknesses," as Yen called them. To accomplish this, he brought Ph.D.s and M.D.s to Ding Xian to collaborate with local people and come up with programs for eliminating poverty and misgovernment—and for establishing and maintaining health throughout Ding Xian. A community would choose a "farmer scholar" to be trained by professionals; he would then test out what he'd learned in various villages, adapting it as needed. This was the beginning of what's now called "evidence-based community development."

This was also where Dr. John B. Grant, a Canadian and the son of Chinese missionaries, a man who, after his death in 1962, was said to have "influenced the health care of half of the people of the world," became part of what had been up to then Jimmy Yen's story. And it is where the concept of primary health care took form.

A member of the first class graduated by the Johns Hopkins School of Public Health, Grant was sent to China by the Rockefeller Foundation in 1921, and he came up with a plan for "medicine for the future," whose central principle was that "any artificial separation of curative and preventive medicine is detrimental to the efficiency of both." Grant dedicated himself to setting up what he called a "real health station" in areas that "combined curative and preventive medicine in a community" and was also a place for training people in both preventive and curative practices based on the specific problems each area faced. Although he didn't use the phrase "primary health care," Grant had already worked out what would be needed to make it effective: M.D.s working as a team with hygiene specialists.

In response to Jimmy Yen's reaching out to him, a pilot health station became part of the Ding Xian Experiment in 1929. It was so successful that, even though the experiment had to be abruptly abandoned in 1937 when the Japanese Army invaded China, Yen's idea for primary health care—or a piece of it, the prevention part—was revived by the Chinese Communist government after it took power in 1949.

In the 1950s, 200,000 Chinese farmers, called "village doctors," were given vaccines to administer, along with some basic medical and first aid training. That way, in their spare time, they could provide preventive medicine to their neighbors and supervise them in "snail control" programs. Parasitic worms living in tiny, freshwater snails were the cause of "big belly," schistosomiasis, a neglected tropical disease that produces distended stomachs, can inflame the liver and spleen, and kills up to 200,000 people a year. These worms had infested ten million Chinese farmers. When many of the swamps the snails lived in were drained, the infection rate plummeted, in some areas by as much as 90 percent.

A decade later, Chairman Mao, who thought six years of medical school were a waste of time when one or two would suffice and who had failed to persuade fully trained urban doctors to move to the countryside, brought half a million farmers to Chinese hospitals for three to six months of instruction in inoculations, wound tending, and medical education (getting people to wash their hands before eating and after going to the bathroom). Then they went home again to be part-time farmers and part-time health workers, taking with them a few medicines, some needles and syringes, and not much else because of lack of funds.

By the mid-1970s there were a million of these "barefoot doctors," as they were known—a term stemming from the centuries-old tradition of southern Chinese farmers who worked barefoot out in the rice paddies. Visiting China in 1973, a leading U.S. physician, Dr. Philip Lee (a former assistant secretary of health), was impressed, saying that the Chinese countryside was a "dramatically different" place than before the Communist revolution and that now that "some health service" was available for most people, infant mortality was down, major epidemic diseases had been controlled, and "massive campaigns of health education and environmental sanitation" were in place.

Dr. Lee's enthusiasm was the prologue to the worldwide gathering in Alma-Ata, Kazakhstan, in 1978, the International Conference on Primary Health Care, when representatives of 134 countries gathered, inspired in large part by the "barefoot doctors." They reasserted Andrija Štampar's ringing 1946 definition of health as a state that moves people far beyond the condition of not being sick; called health "a fundamental human right"; endorsed primary health care as "scientifically sound" and affordable by every country; linked its achievement to the eradication of poverty and social inequality; and, in the Declaration of Alma-Ata, unanimously and dramatically proclaimed to the world a goal for humanity: "Health for All People by the Year 2000."

But what came next was a turning away from Yen's vision, a postponement that would last decades. Even before Alma-Ata, which briefly glowed as a triumphant moment, there had been twists in the path. In the postwar period, as primary health care was being greatly scaled up—a million "barefoot doctors"!—it was also dramatically scaled back, becoming "focused," as a bulletin put out by the World Health Organization (WHO) noted, "on prevention rather than cures."

Looking back at the Alma-Ata Conference several years later, many people found it hard to characterize. Had it been a shining moment, a polestar to navigate by? Had it come and gone like heat lightning? Had there been a "sublime consensus," in the words of the magnetic Dr. Halfdan Mahler, son of a Danish preacher and WHO's director in those years, "between the haves and have-nots in global health"? Or maybe it had all been wishful thinking and the idea of making primary health care the key strategy that would "enable all people without exception" (Mahler's words) "to live socially and economically productive lives" was simply too heavy a load for the world to lift then.

The conference's definition of primary health care—though linked to countries developing parallel programs in farming, industry, and housing to create "a whole new way of life" since "medical care alone cannot bring health to hovels"—was modest enough. Its focus was on how to stay healthy and on preventing diseases with immunizations, and it emphasized proper care for mothers and young children and what was called "appropriate treatment for common diseases." It advocated public health programs for better nutrition and clean drinking water. Perhaps in the interest of arriving at unanimity within the few days available, it didn't spell out who in any country would be involved in making this happen, but the assumption seemed to be that the bulk of it would be handled by teams of workers with at least some paramedical training.

In the run-up to the conference, some groups had expressed hostility to hospitals, calling them "basically repair facilities which did little if anything to remove the causes of sickness or to promote and maintain health." There were crosscurrents at work: general dissatisfaction with WHO's earlier "vertical" programs, meaning campaigns to eliminate single diseases. There had been one spectacular success—smallpox eradication in 1980—but the Global Malaria Eradication Program had been abandoned after fourteen years because of the stubborn persistence of the disease in sub-Saharan Africa. "Horizontal" programs, on the other hand, try to address all the health problems affecting an area.

At the same time, many newly independent countries (Kazakhstan itself was not yet an independent nation but a subordinate part of the Soviet Union) were trying to reinvent health services that had been designed by and for now-displaced colonial elites— a situation that Cold War adversaries wanted to take advantage of. In this case, not the U.S.S.R. and the U.S., the most prominent rivals, but the rivals within the "Socialist Camp," as they called themselves: the U.S.S.R. and China. Behind the scenes, Moscow offered the WHO two million dollars to organize an international conference because, as their representative candidly admitted, they could "not permit a Chinese victory" in the health practices that would be adopted by third-world countries.

The city of Alma-Ata, now called Almaty, is less than two hundred miles west of China—and China was the one major country that did not attend the Alma-Ata Conference. The conference had a Soviet look to it; it was convened in the Lenin

Palace, an enormous auditorium with a curiously curved golden roof that looked like a serving platter for canapés incongruously perched on top. The building seated three thousand and was modeled on the vast Lenin Palace in Moscow, which was built in Khrushchev's time for Communist Party Congresses. Alma-Ata, the largest city in Kazakhstan, which before the Bolshevik Revolution had been a small farming town (the city's name means "grandfather of apples"), was essentially a prolonged Soviet-era construction project that lasted into the 1970s, with four-lane highways and a skyline of oversized, sculpted concrete and so-called "Soviet Modernism" buildings, including a high-rise thousand-room hotel put up the year before the conference.

Despite the Soviet look, the conference did not have a Soviet feel. Participants remembered a "kind of jubilation" in the vast hall and a conviction that they were part of a historic development. People had tears in their eyes when, on the final day, an African doctor, a young woman in flowing robes, read the text of the Declaration out loud. Mahler called it a "sacred moment," the result of "an overwhelming feeling that 'we must arrive at a consensus.'"

My souvenir for Gaus was nothing more than previously unknown film footage from the conference. When I'd first seen it, it had surprised me and stayed with me. In a startlingly vivid and moving way, it captured the essence of that might-have-been or almost-was occasion. It gave me a chance to observe the excitement those three thousand delegates had felt (even without the Chinese, they represented sixty-seven international organizations as well as the 134 countries in attendance), caught up in the thought that "Health for All" could be achieved in less than a generation.

As an object the film was a trifling thing, a DVD, playable on any laptop, something a friend who'd recently visited Kazakhstan had picked up—a high-quality copy of a long-forgotten, Soviet-era, Russian-language official newsreel in black and white that had been widely shown in Kazakh movie theaters the month after the conference. And then it had disappeared. Another friend, who speaks Russian, had walked me through the stilted narration, which I was now prepared to do for Gaus.

The conference is the lead item of four news stories and gets six full minutes. At this forty-year remove, the remainder of the newsreel feels unbelievably dated and silly, a relic of another world. There are two minutes about the 1978 Kazakh grain harvest (the year's best combine drivers are presented with wreaths made of wheat stalks, while their bumper harvest is attributed to wise decisions made by the Communist Party). Then, after a minute spent praising Kazakhstan's leading mining foreman, whose work has also been given new purpose by the Party, there's an all-smiles, wrap-up minute about "a very exciting event," an ice-hockey game between Kazakhstan and Bulgaria, at the time a Soviet satellite ("of course, friendship won").

Yet this was the context within which the Alma-Ata conference flowered. The only speaker whose voice can actually be heard on the DVD is that of the first secretary of the Kazakh Communist Party, wearing his three Gold Star Hero of Soviet Labor medals. In a wooden tone, he reads a speech by Leonid Brezhnev about how, under the guidance of the Communist Party, every citizen of the U.S.S.R. enjoys free medical care.

The repeated glimpses of the delegates themselves are what bring the conference back to life—first as they're welcomed at the airport with flowers while stirring music plays, then as they talk animatedly in small groups in the Lenin Palace lobby and fill almost every seat in the auditorium, listening intently to speakers from around the world. You see them getting to know one another on carefully arranged field trips to the Kazakh Institute of Oncology and Radiation and to a small, freestanding primary health care clinic that looks even newer than the conference hotel. You watch them warmly applaud the surprise guest, Sen. Ted Kennedy, who turned up unexpectedly the first day to hail "Health for All" as a "truly noble goal" and to call the conference "a unique event"—nations, he said (his words are pieced together from a press release I found online), "brought together not to discuss high technology, not to discuss bricks and mortar, not to discuss technical ideas—but rather to discuss a basic human right—the right of every man, woman, and child to health care."

In the newsreel we never see the young African doctor reading the Alma-Ata Declaration out loud. Instead we're told that the final speaker was the Soviet minister of health, a surgeon famous for having performed the first successful kidney transplant in the U. S. S. R. Still, there's an inescapable sense that something out of the ordinary, perhaps monumental, has been unfolding.

CHAPTER THIRTEEN

ROSY AFTERGLOW
AND COLD,
HARD DAWN

MIGHT HAVE BEEN. ALMOST WAS. HALFDAN MAHLER, deeply disappointed when he looked back on the aftermath of the "Health for All" Alma-Ata Conference, began calling what followed "Hell for All" and a "counter-revolution" and said that the world had gone "right back to square one."

But the Declaration of Alma-Ata had been an exhortation and an outline of a health strategy, not a detailed plan for a health system. It had announced to the world that humanity knew enough to get started on a global program to lay down for all time what for the past quarter century has been called "the global burden of disease," which measures the gap between how healthy people actually are and (as one definition puts it) the "ideal situation where everyone lives into old age, free of disease and disability." But the Declaration had been drawn up as a nonbinding resolution, with no funding to make things happen.

Some countries committed themselves wholeheartedly to primary health care and have remained so. Confusingly, a couple of the most successful of these national programs get little attention in North America because of tense and mistrustful relationships and a history of vehement disagreements between the United States and the revolutionary regimes funding them: the Islamic Republic of Iran and Fidel Castro's Cuba.

Iran has thirty-one thousand *behvarzan* (which means people with "good-skills" in Persian) who monitor the health of the rural population from seventeen thousand "health houses" in villages around the country (usually there's a man and a woman *behvarz* in each one). Recruited from their communities, *behvarzan* keep a logbook of each family known to them, have a limited supply of drugs, and refer any complicated cases to a district health center with an M.D. They're paraprofessionals, or they could be called health auxiliaries; they're specialized paramedics with a high school education and two years of training as community health workers (CHWs for short, an acronym gaining popularity as a catch-all term for the most primary of primary health care workers). The Iranian *behvarzan* have been credited with cutting infant mortality in half and maternal mortality by three-quarters while also getting 95 percent of the country immunized, up from 20 percent.

Immediately after the 1959 Cuban revolution, half the country's six thousand doctors emigrated, mostly to the United States. The island now has ninety thousand physicians, nineteen thousand of whom work abroad, and thirty-one thousand who staff free neighborhood medical centers at home, assisted by a nurse. "There are too many doctors," exclaimed one incredulous foreign visitor. "Everybody has a family physician." Annual physical exams are mandatory, and the neighborhood doctors will track down anyone who doesn't show up. The training level of these doctors, though far more advanced than that of a *behvarz*, is somewhere between that of a U.S. physician and a practical nurse. Because of the 1962 U.S. embargo on trade with Cuba, they have had to make do with antiquated equipment and a constant shortage of supplies and medicines, from aspirins to antibiotics.

Not much discussed is that fact that these neighborhood doctors sometimes act as informal government agents, passing on nonmedical information about their patients' habits and activities to various authorities. Their achievements, nevertheless, are considerable. Cuban and U.S. life expectancies are nearly identical (78.55 versus 79); the Cuban infant mortality rate is lower than the U.S. rate. Visiting Havana in 2014, Dr. Margaret Cho, Halfdan Mahler's most recent successor as WHO director general, said: "We sincerely hope that all of the world's inhabitants will have access to quality medical services, as they do in Cuba."

The Chinese "barefoot doctor" program that had inspired Alma-Ata, the *behvarzan* in Iran, and the neighborhood doctors in Cuba foundered three years after the conference. The "doctors" had been paid by China's collective farms, but with the introduction of "market forces," the land was privatized, and once the barefoot doctors lost their income, their patients had no one to turn to.

But the most profound departure from the spirit of Alma-Ata came when UNICEF, the United Nations Children's Fund, a cosponsor of Alma-Ata, threw its weight behind what came to be called the "children survival revolution." It was a simple, cheap, but narrowed-down alternative to primary health care called "selective primary health care." Originally put forward as an "interim" solution, it focused exclusively on infants and their mothers. The acronym it introduced—GOBI-FFF—refers to seven interventions that are easy to administer.

The "O," for instance, stands for oral rehydration to combat diarrhea, now only the second leading (rather than the leading) cause of death in young children in developing countries, the result of contaminated food and water. Diarrhea still kills three million children a year under the age of one, but GOBI's "O" is credited with having saved forty million lives. "O" preparation is simple: Add a packet of dried salts and sugars to water and give a small child a teaspoonful every two or three minutes. The "B" in GOBI is for breastfeeding. The "I" is for immunizations; by 1990, through a strategy of "national days of immunization," UNICEF had vaccinated 80 percent of the kids in developing countries against TB, polio, measles, diphtheria, tetanus, and whooping cough, the six basic childhood diseases.

Ironically, the great champion of the children survival revolution was Dr. James P. Grant, son of Dr. John B. Grant, who in China sixty years earlier had come up with the original comprehensive approach to primary health care. Jim Grant was as compelling a figure as Mahler or Jimmy Yen, and, according to Grant's biographer, he "cajoled and persuaded and flattered and shamed and praised" every head of state he met, whether that meant he "shook hands that were stained with blood, hands that had turned the keys on political prisoners, hands that had signed away human rights, hands that were deep in the country's till." Criticized by some for concentrating on "short-term benefits" that are "only a Band-Aid solution to the lack of clean water and modern sanitation in many poor settings," Grant had, according to New York Times columnist Nicholas Kristof, "probably saved more lives than were destroyed by Hitler, Mao and Stalin combined," and in 1994 Grant was awarded the Presidential Medal of Freedom by President Bill Clinton.

So the legacy of Alma-Ata seemed to combine rosy afterglow and cold, hard dawn. Although on the "vertical" side (campaigns against individual diseases) there have been some breaks in the clouds: Since 2000, an enormous amount of government and private money has been spent to stop the spread of HIV/AIDS, TB, malaria, and other diseases including, most notably, President George W. Bush's multi-billion-dollar PEPFAR (President's Emergency Plan for AIDS Relief).

PEPFAR has been called "the largest health initiative ever initiated by one country to address a disease," and it's estimated that it has saved 1.1 million lives in Africa. The Bill and Melinda Gates Foundation, created in 2000 by the world's richest man, now spends as much each year on these vertical health programs (over $1 billion) as WHO does, in addition to devoting $2 billion a year to anti-poverty programs (such as those offering vaccinations, polio elimination, infant health, and efforts to make water cleaner and farmland more productive). Bill Gates has given the foundation $30 billion, and Warren Buffett, the world's third-richest man, has pledged to match that amount. They plan to have spent all this money within twenty years of Bill and Melinda Gates's deaths (presumably within the twenty-first century; he was born in 1955, and she is nine years younger).

The Gateses have said they expect that between now and 2030, the lives of people in developing countries will improve faster than "at any other time in history" and their lives "will improve more than anyone else's." They call this "our big bet" and say, "It's great that more people in rich countries will be able to watch movies on super hi-resolution screens. It's even better that more people in poor countries will know their children aren't going to die."

Meanwhile, though, over a billion of the 7.5 billion people in the world do not have access to basic health services; the drawback to "vertical," or disease-specific, medical programs is that they create their own bureaucracies and bring little funding for other health issues. According to WHO, there should already be 7.9 million more health care workers in addition to the world's 15 million doctors. WHO's assumption is that the "basic threshold" for adequate health care is "23 skilled health professionals per 10,000 people." WHO projects that things will only get worse because "not enough young people are entering the profession or being adequately trained." If, as expected, the global population hits 8.8 billion by 2035, there would then be a shortage of 12.9 million health care workers.

Unfortunately, what has been carried forward from Alma-Ata is the wide separation between the work to stop people from getting sick and the efforts to treat them once they get sick—that is, between preventive and curative medicine, the linked approach that John B. Grant had recommended to Jimmy Yen as the most effective way to bring health to an area. In valedictory remarks about Alma-Ata that Halfdan Mahler made before the Sixty-first World Health Assembly in 2008, he reminded his listeners, on the thirtieth anniversary of the conference, never to "forget that visionaries have been the realists in human progression."

Had anyone since Alma-Ata tried to do a "Jimmy Yen" or a "John B. Grant" and reconcile these twin components of health? Even in a small way? Yes, one such visionary—Dr. Carroll Behrhorst, known as "Doc," a U.S. family medicine doctor from Kansas. He spent thirty years working with the Maya-Kaqchikel people in the highlands of rural Guatemala, one of the few areas in Latin America where direct descendants of the pre-Colombian population still make up three quarters of the people. "He had Viking blue eyes, sun-bleached, straw-blond hair, and a healthy corpulence," a visiting American physician said of Behrhorst. "He moved with the drive of a Kansas wheat farmer bringing in the harvest before the storm," and "he addressed you forthrightly, right to the soul." Other visitors noted the "twang, bounce, and jubilance in his speech." Uniquely, Carroll Behrhorst was someone Mahler deeply admired, someone whose work had begun long before Alma-Ata and continued well after it—and someone whose story touched the life of David Gaus. In his last years, Behrhorst became a mentor to Gaus, then a medical student in New Orleans who up to then had never heard of Alma-Ata.

In a posthumous tribute to Behrhorst, who died in 1990, Mahler called him "a healer of many schisms: between the science of medicine and the art of medicine, between medicine and health, between prevention and cure, between health and development"— and many more, including "between sympathy and empathy."

In 1960, when Behrhorst arrived in Chimaltenango, thirty miles west of Guatemala City and then a town of 20,000, he found that the Kaqchikel, 140,000 modern-day Mayans, lived in high, farmed valleys surrounded by mountains and towering volcanoes—and had practically no medical facilities. What they did have was a profound sense of the importance of health, linking it to "the performance of positive functions: a good appetite, hard work, enjoyment of nature, and participation in the village." One woman explained that because Mayans see themselves as part of nature—"We both give sense to the land and receive sense from the land"—anything that disrupts this balance is unhealthy.

Behrhorst built what he called a *hospitalito* in Chimaltenango with seventy beds and a clinic. He treated a hundred patients in a morning and made a point of charging at least a few pennies for each service; he had learned that the Kaqchikel consider free medicine worthless. Outside Chimaltenango, he trained "health promoters" who lived in the surrounding villages, where poverty and severe malnutrition were exacerbated by the fact that 80 percent of the farmland belonged to only 2 percent of the people.

He visited the health promoters regularly during what his associates remembered as "bone-crushing rides" in a battered red Jeep that showed his "disciplined madness" behind the wheel; he "loved those drives" said friends, "and that's where he talked most freely." Like the "barefoot doctors" in China, the Kaqchikel health promoters were trained to do simple things, like washing hands and boiling water, and to treat common diseases with some drugs—"seventy-five to 80 percent of all illnesses," Behrhorst told an interviewer, "are self-limiting. Too often the doctor takes credit for nature's work."

Loan funds were set up to help farmers buy fertilizer, pesticides, and better seeds, and there was a foundation that could purchase farmland from any landowner willing to sell. It was a hybrid "Health for All" model set up long before the idea had become a phrase or a movement—and it showed its strength and effectiveness after a crippling 3 a.m. earthquake in 1976 killed twenty-three thousand people and wounded seventy-seven thousand (who among them sustained fifty-five thousand bone fractures in a single half-minute, according to a Denver M.D.).

Behrhorst called the earthquake "the earth's undoing," but his hospital, built of steel and concrete, was one of the few buildings in Chimaltenango to survive the quake. As reporters flocked to Guatemala, where a quarter of a million homes had been destroyed along with two-fifths of the hospitals, Behrhorst and his staff and health promoters gained international recognition as "the best organized medical team in the country." Some took to calling Behrhorst the "Schweitzer of the New World," and in the run-up to Alma-Ata, WHO called his work "one of the ten models worldwide for effective health promotion."

Even so, over the long run the Chimaltenango program got battered by Guatemala's unrelenting civil war, which dated back to 1960, the year Behrhorst had arrived in the country. In 1980, violence between government security forces and guerilla forces reached the highlands, destroying four hundred villages. Behrhorst's hospital stayed open, treating the wounded from both sides of the struggle, but thirty-two of his forty-seven health promoters were killed. He called this "a devastating experience."

Behrhorst moved his family to the United States, though he still made regular visits to Guatemala. He began teaching at the Tulane School of Public Health and Tropical Medicine—where several years later David Gaus became one of his students. In 1986, Behrhorst continued to look forward, writing of his program, "We dream that it will eventually become an accepted structure in Guatemala, akin to the volcanoes," and "a self-supporting system independent of all foreign help, including my own, and relying totally on native nurses and doctors," an organization "moving by its own lights and on its own feet into the next century."

Talk about Schweitzer always made Behrhorst uneasy—since he found the idea of "white knights" who would ride in from afar to solve or save things a "debasing image." "I'm just a country doctor," he insisted.

CHAPTER FOURTEEN

FAMILY MEDICINE

"ONLY THAT DAY DAWNS TO WHICH WE ARE AWAKE."
This is a Thoreau quote from the last paragraph of *Walden* and
one of the greetings Carroll Behrhorst sent in letters to friends
around the world. It stuck in my head when I had the chance to
talk to Gaus about Behrhorst on a drive to Pedro, the original,
smaller AHD hospital. The subject came up naturally enough
since there were striking similarities in the ways the two men be-
haved on the road—not only in the ways they drove but in how
they considered long rides a good chance to talk. Gaus said:

> I met Carroll Behrhorst my second year in medical school.
> It was the last spring of his life—he had a heart attack that
> May. Had he lived I would've spent that summer in Chi-
> maltenango. I was taking medical microbiology, a two- or
> three-week session on parasitology. Because Behrhorst was
> a down-to-earth, salt-of-the-earth kind of guy, humble, so

unlike a remote university professor, he encouraged me to visit him and drill him with questions. I was fascinated. He had that kind of glow about him that people get when they've given their lives to something worthwhile, like creating health. People who don't expect things to be handed to them. People who, when they're told "No," hear it as "Not yet."

A lot of things that became bedrock ideas with me first came up in those talks with Behrhorst, such as the idea that anything I set up would have to be self-sustaining if it was to be of any use and have a chance to last. His whole principle was "for Guatemalans, by Guatemalans." It would've helped him to have more Guatemalan doctors, not just the health promoters, and when no doctors were around, he did all the inpatient work himself. Which made it harder for him to do what he wanted to do, which was fade into the background and not be seen as the indispensable person. Luckily, as a family physician he had an unusual array of skills. Exactly the type of doctor I would need to put on our team in Ecuador to have a full staff, not separate pediatricians, internists, and ob/gyns. And if these family physicians were also accompanied by general surgeons with adequate ob/gyn training, we could keep C-section rates below 25 percent, for instance. In private Ecuadorian clinics, the rate is over 70 percent, which U.S. doctors call well within the "crazy range"—it's what happens when doctors want to create volume.

We were rolling along past big banana tree plantations that looked as though they dated back to the days when Hólger Velasteguí first broadcast about the good land near Santo that was waiting for good farmers. On this Correa-refurbished highway, I was getting the hang of how these roads operate. Who uses what lane is not entirely established—it's something of a transitional moment. The traffic is a constant mix of trucks doing about 25 miles an hour and cars doing 60. The road's instructions to drivers are for the most part transmitted by tactile means—through a system of jarring, can't-be-ignored rumble strips. Approaching a pedestrian crossing there's a series of progressively wider strips, then a narrow speed bump, and then a wider one. Approaching a *zona escolar* (school zone) there are three strips of equal width. Occasionally everything has to slow down when a lane has been closed for repaving—*asfalto fresco* (fresh asphalt). Then a traditional Ecuador reasserts itself: Even with no village visible within miles, people form small groups along the road to sell *papas* and *bebidas* (potato chips and drinks).

"Family medicine?" Gaus said. "How to describe it—here's a good analogy from William Ventres, who worked in Venezuela in the 1990s." Ventres was a U.S. physician and medical anthropologist. "He remembered that Subcommandante Marcos, the spokesman for the indigenous Zapatista uprising in southern Mexico during those years, wore one watch on his left arm set to Mexican time, and another on his right arm set an hour ahead, to Zapatista time, as a way of saying that the Zapatista ideas of equity and democracy were an hour ahead of Mexican reality. So Ventres did the same thing, with the watch on his left arm representing medicine as it is, and the watch on his right 'bearing the time of family medicine, one hour ahead.'" That hour, Ventres later wrote, is "the time that family physicians work with their patients collaboratively and caringly, attacking and preventing disease, overcoming disability, and facing life's difficulties."

Rumble—rumble—rumble. We slowed down. A *zona escolar.* Gaus said:

Family physicians have been called the Swiss Army knives of medicine. A family physician, or family medicine doctor, is a specialist who, like all medical specialists, has been through three years of a residency program after medical school, and thus begins her work life having completed seven years of training. Specialization became the norm after World War II, when suddenly there was so much more to know. Theoretically, all specialists know more about something—kidneys, lungs—than you do, but a family medicine doctor has more arrows in the quiver and not just a single, beautiful arrow.

Her watch is set an hour ahead, because learning family medicine is more than just doing more hospital rotations than you did in med school. It's going deeper into the whole field and along the way acquiring a different point of view.

In the 1970s, when family medicine was still new, a psychiatrist named George Engle introduced the biopsychosocial—BPS—model of medicine. This says that to understand what's happening to a person, you need to know more than viruses and bacteria and genes, the biomedical model, and be ready to understand how people are affected by their state of mind and the state of their family and community. You have to take in a whole lot more territory, and you have to be nimble about it.

Rumble—RUMBLE—bump—*bump*. A pedestrian crossing, though no one was in sight. We stopped and then picked up speed again. Gaus continued:

I remember as an undergrad, I had a management professor named Fr. Dave Tyson who talked about the difference between doing a thing right and doing the right thing. Or, as he put it, between efficient action and effective action. For instance, you have a patient with belly pain. A gastroenterologist might do a gastroscopy—use a thin, flexible tube to look through the esophagus and stomach and small intestine, and they might do it very well. But did they do the right thing? Not everyone with belly pain needs a tube down the stomach to see what's happening. A family physician might check the liver and the gallbladder, figure out the belly pain that way, give medicine, and the patient feels better. Family doctors aren't gatekeepers—a condescending term, someone who tells you, "You need to go to this or that specialist." They're not triage nurses, who send you on to definitive treatment. One WHO doctor calls them five-star doctors, because they can handle so many variables all at once and by themselves. Since 2008, Diego and I have been telling people at the Ministry of Public Health that it was time for Ecuador to recognize family medicine as a specialty, because what this country needs is a team of family medicine doctors—an idea they finally bought into, realizing that these were the ideal people for outpatient clinics and rural hospitals.

Also in 2008, which happened to be the thirtieth anniversary of Alma-Ata, Gaus wrote a paper in the spirit of the conference called "Making Secondary Care a Primary Concern: The Rural Hospital in Ecuador." Gaus wrote it with Diego Herrera and several U.S. doctors, including Dr. Barnett L. Cline, one of Gaus's teachers, and Dr. Julius Richmond, one of AHD's most prominent early backers. Richmond, then 92, was a pediatrician who'd been a vice admiral in the United States Public Health Service and surgeon general during the Carter administration, and also the first director of the Head Start program, which since the 1960s has helped 22 million low-income preschoolers. The paper described the services at Hospital Pedro Vicente Maldonado and called "rural secondary-care hospitals (RSCHs)" that were staffed by family physicians "the missing link," able to "provide local care for the vast majority of all medical needs in rural communities."

Gaus and Herrera have said that, as the "middle piece" of a national health care system, small rural hospitals can handle the twenty most common causes of hospitalization, including pneumonia and pregnancy complications, can set broken bones, and can perform the most common surgeries as well, such as appendectomies and C-sections (when necessary), once the family physicians have the services of a general surgeon (HPVM has one on staff five days a week).

They also point out that secondary hospitals out in the countryside take the pressure off tertiary hospitals in the big cities, where the same routine procedures, such as taking out an appendix, are far more expensive. But family physicians are the centerpiece inside this middle piece: they compress everything down to the doable and the affordable. They're not surgeons—that is, they're not six-star doctors—but they're multifunctional and can do the work of internists, pediatricians, and ob/gyns.

The following year, on the strength of Gaus's paper, he and Herrera were invited to present their views at a WHO meeting in Rio de Janeiro on the role of district hospitals in primary care. Other participants in that 2010 conference, Gaus noted afterward, seemed more focused on traditional remedies, such as providing clean water to rural villages. "I was speaking Greek," he said. "They were speaking Latin." These days he sounds more optimistic. In a recent Skype call from Santo, Gaus said he saw signs that "the bigger discussion," meaning the one on the role of hospitals in primary health care, was finally getting started. He said:

> The door is opening. There's the classic argument against a hospital, that it sucks up money and postpones action. But a hospital doesn't have to be expensive. The IESS, the Ecuadorian Social Security Administration, built a hundred-bed hospital in Santo at about the same time we built our sixty-bed Hospital Hesburgh. Theirs cost $25 million, ours $5 million. We don't have subspecialty care—there's no plastic surgery, heart surgery, or neurosurgery. But we can take care of pneumonia, a kidney infection, bad asthma attacks, a highway accident, snakebites. A hospital can't stand alone, but our position is that when you create small, cost-effective hospitals as an essential part of a country's health care, you actually accelerate the arrival of health in communities. Otherwise the emphasis on prevention, promotion, and education loses credibility. Why? Because people still get sick even so, and if you can't help them when they're suffering, you'll lose them on the other side.

Diego Herrera joined Gaus on camera and said, "If people don't have confidence in your abilities, that you know what you're doing, that you can help them heal, a prevention-promotion-education program will fall on deaf ears. It's a little bit unorthodox to say this, but one reason we strongly believe in curative services is that if someone gets pneumonia, and two days later they're feeling better, you have a lot more credibility and legitimacy. Then, when they go home, they're much more likely to have their kids vaccinated."

Gaus said:

I remember how it was before we built Hospital Pedro Vicente Maldonado. This is before I realized we *needed* to build that hospital. A woman named Maria, who lived deep in the countryside, came to the small clinic I'd set up. She heard me talking to some of the women in Pedro about the danger signs of preeclampsia. "Doc," Maria said, "if we get these symptoms, where should we go?" I still only had primary health care thinking, and suggested she go to the Ministry of Public Health outpatient clinic. I knew they hadn't been trained in preeclampsia management and that magnesium sulfate, the drug that works, usually wasn't even on the shelves. And I told her she might have to make a trip all the way to Quito. She could sense my frustration even during the pep talk, because what she said then was, "So why tell us about this disease if there's nothing you can do for us?"

She made a strong impression on me, I can tell you. I later wrote her up in one of my first articles. I think if the primary health care debate were to start from scratch today, a lot more people would see it this way. For one thing, to be helpful and effective—and remember, being effective is more useful than being efficient—you've got to know what diseases you're up against and you need that curative component for when people get sick. It's the only way to build a healthy health care system—a system that people will be willing to plug into and trust.

CHAPTER FIFTEEN

FATHER TED

HOW WAS IT THAT GAUS AND HIS TEAM WERE ABLE TO learn Greek, and why is it such a rarity? In William Ventres's terminology, why don't more people set their watches an hour ahead? As Dr. Michael Heisler, a critical care internist who's been part of AHD's advisory board since 1999, says, what makes Andean Health and Development capable of "dealing with the big, big questions history is working with"?

One night in my room, I discovered something Jimmy Yen had written, his sharpest insight—in poetic form, not that of a manifesto:

Go to the people.
Live with the people.
Plan with the people.
Work with the people.
Start with what they know.

Build on what they have.
Teach by showing, learn by doing.
Not a showcase, but a pattern.
Not piecemeal, but integrated.
Not odds and ends, but a system.
Not to conform, but to transform.
Not relief, but release.

Just inside the front door of Hospital Hesburgh, there's a short prayer that's part of a mural:

Señor, dad pan a los que tienen hambre, y a los que si tienen pan, dadles hambre de justicia.

This translates as

Lord, give bread to those who are hungry, and to those who have bread, give them a hunger for justice.

It's a prayer that seems to have universal authorship—it's been attributed to the Benedictines, to the Chinese, and to Saint Oscar Romero of El Salvador, a beloved champion of the poor who was assassinated in 1980 while saying Mass. It was also the favorite grace before meals of the man for whom Hospital Hesburgh is named, the Rev. Theodore M. Hesburgh, the revered Catholic priest who was president of the University of Notre Dame for thirty-five years. Among many, many other titles and honors—he was considered the most honored man of his generation, with 150 honorary degrees from colleges and universities on five continents—he was also president of the AHD Advisory Board for over twenty years, stepping down only a few months before his death in 2015 at the age of 97.

It was, notably, the very last of his many board memberships, one that came to mean more and more to him as he got older. Fr. John Jenkins, the current president of Notre Dame, in his eulogy at Hesburgh's funeral on campus, mentioned David

Gaus by name when discussing the hundreds of people whose lives Hesburgh had touched, telling Gaus, who was sitting in the congregation, "You continued his work." When Gaus later wrote Fr. Jenkins to thank him for his courtesy, Jenkins wrote back: "I had to. I must have heard that story from Fr. Ted 20 to 30 times."

Father Ted, as he liked to be called, a handsome man who combined Irish charm and German discipline (his family had come from both countries), was famous for many things: for his ferocious intellect and insatiable curiosity; for speaking Greek and Latin and eight other languages; for having traveled three million miles on visits to 130 countries; for having transformed Notre Dame, as it was said, from being the Catholic West Point (a school that had been, as he acknowledged, a "sluggish, tradition-bound university" with a lingering reputation as a "football factory") into the Catholic Princeton, renowned for its academics as well as for fielding a formidable football team. Above all he loved being a priest, his ambition since boyhood, and seemed buoyed and sustained, cradled and liberated, by his priestly vows of poverty and obedience, saying you had a lot of time to think if you weren't distracted by money or sex or having to advance your career.

Friends remembered him as someone who was at once firmly anchored and constantly evolving. Looking back on his college presidency, which began when he was 35, he said: "I took those first six years like a hundred-yard dash; then when I got to the tape I had to keep going. I'd have been bored to death if all I did was be president of the university. Once you've been through it six times, you pretty much know where all the holes in the road are." But, he added, "When you're young and do everything halfway decently, you get asked to do something else. I could always do three or four jobs at the same time."

The things he got asked to do included serving on sixteen presidential commissions under nine U.S. presidents. He chaired the Civil Right Commission from 1957 to 1972 and has been called the architect of the Civil Rights Act of 1964. He was also chairman of the Rockefeller Foundation and president of the Harvard Board of Overseers. He championed what he and his biographer,

Michael O'Brien, called dual citizenship, meaning forming a commitment to the country of your birth and to the world, pledging "ourselves, our lives, whatever talent or time we possess, to do something about the monumental injustices that exist." He called the community service that Notre Dame students performed a "new sacrament," saying, "They may, if they walk this path, find a deeper and more realistic spirituality than we found. Perhaps they will avoid the dichotomy of the pious person who was totally lacking in a hunger for justice or compassion for the poor of the world."

Fr. Hesburgh's goal of transforming Notre Dame came to him, he said, "silently, as a kind of vision," shortly after he was named president: "I envisioned Notre Dame as a great Catholic university, the greatest in the world! Not since the Middle Ages had there been a great Catholic university." Along the way, he put up forty new buildings on campus, including a fourteen-story library (at the time the largest college library in the world) that has the university's third spire, the other two being the bell tower of the Basilica of the Sacred Heart, the campus church, and the famous Gold Dome on the old Main Building, which dates to 1882.

The library, now named for Hesburgh, was a monumental way of showing that the focus of the university had expanded to include an equal emphasis on intellectual values. Hesburgh was proud of the fact that the library cost more than a new Athletic Convocation Center and that work on it began before much of the money had been raised. Mike Heisler, a Notre Dame grad (class of 1971) who knew Fr. Ted for forty-five years, loves to tell the "library story" as a quick way of introducing Hesburgh to people who never knew him: "The old library dated back to the First World War and held 100,000 books, so the architect for the new library sat down with Fr. Ted and said, 'I assume you'd like to double that, to 200,000 books?' Fr. Ted said, 'You can start by doubling that.' '400,000, then? Or . . . what figure do you have in mind?' 'Six million.' 'Maybe that's too big?' 'Too small. But we'll start with six million, and leave room to double it.'"

I must have heard Mike Heisler tell that story at least a dozen times. For me it illuminates what was perhaps the most unusual quality of Fr. Ted, a man remarkable in the ways he was remarkable—his ability to live in the future without neglecting the present, to live, that is, as if the future had already happened. Where had such a quality come from?

I got a chance to visit Fr. Ted in his large, book-lined office on the thirteenth floor of Hesburgh Library, with a view of the Golden Dome and the basilica. He put down the cigar he was smoking and took me to a small alcove just outside the office so he could show me a framed picture of Fr. Edward Sorin, the young French missionary priest who founded Notre Dame in 1844, when he was 28. In October 1842, the bishop of Vincennes, Indiana, offered Sorin 524 forested acres three hundred miles to the north if he would found a college there within two years. He and his companions set off "in the cold, snow, and high winds," as a Notre Dame archival website records, "with all the gear loaded on a broken-down ox-drawn wagon." There were five feet of snow, and it took Sorin and his party twelve days to reach South Bend, a small village, where he borrowed a horse to travel the final two miles, too impatient to wait until morning to get to the site of the school, his Université de Notre Dame du Lac, then only three log cabins and two frozen lakes.

"And that's the key," Fr. Ted said, near the picture of Fr. Sorin, a determined-looking, unsmiling, bearded man. "It was going to be a one-room school to begin with, and when it did open, in 1844, he had grade-school classes and a trade school and maybe only a dozen college students. He could have said *école*, an elementary school, or *lycée*, more like a high school. I had some big dreams when I became president of Notre Dame, but they pale in comparison with those of Fr. Sorin when he arrived here through the woods and moved into one of the log cabins. Because what he said was, 'On this site we will build the best Catholic university in the New Land.'"

What was called the "crowning moment" of Sorin's life came years later, when he was 65. Fire destroyed the university's original Main Building, and there was a somber gathering in the college church. An eyewitness remembered: "I was then present when Fr. Sorin, after looking over the destruction of his lifework, stood at the altar steps of the only building left and spoke to the community what I have always felt to be the most sublime words I ever listened to. There was absolute faith, confidence, resolution in his very look and pose. 'If it were ALL gone, I should not give up!' were his words in closing. The effect was electric." The present Main Building was built that summer, as three hundred workmen completed what a university historian has called an "architectural marathon" in just over three months. The Golden Dome was added several years later.

Hesburgh celebrated the outcome of the Second Vatican Council in the 1960s, which proclaimed that the church, rather than seeing itself as a fortress of faith, should "ever look to the present," in the words of Pope John XXIII, "to the new conditions and the new forms of life introduced into the modern world." Hesburgh later said, "Having lived half my life before Vatican II, I much prefer the half I have lived since then." The Council, which had assembled 2,500 bishops at St. Peter's Basilica in Rome, had done more than just change the way the church went about its work on a day-to-day basis (letting priests, for instance, celebrate Mass in their own language instead of Latin). It had introduced "openness," making the church "more ready to serve than to control others," and had "brought to a new level the vocation of the laity," the ordinary members of congregations.

Hesburgh's doctoral thesis in 1945 extolled the wisdom of the laity; decades before that, in Belgium and France, the "Jocists," the *Jeunesse ouvrière chrétienne* (lay groups of Young Christian Workers), had sought to bring the presence of the Church directly into modern factories, urging workers to think for themselves about how to change their situation. Don't consult scripture first, they said. Instead—"observe, judge, act."

On the eve of World War II, the Jocists had half a million followers in Europe. Their founder, Abbé Joseph Cardijn, a short, passionate Belgian priest with a crew cut who, near the end of his life, was made a prince of the Church and called the "workers' cardinal," had said that his purpose had always been "reconciling the church with the industrial workers of the world." The same *Méthode Jociste*, to observe, judge, and act rather than react according to preconceptions, was later adopted by liberation theology community-action groups in Latin America as a way of challenging centuries of poverty. Fr. Gustavo Gutiérrez, the Peruvian theologian and former medical student who became a founder of liberation theology in the 1970s, famously called this reorienting of the church a "preferential option for the poor."

CHAPTER SIXTEEN

THE BIG STUFF

ANDEAN HEALTH AND DEVELOPMENT DRAWS ITS INFLUENCE
from all corners of the globe, if most closely from Fr. Theodore
M. Hesburgh:

> Go to the people.
> Not to conform, but to transform.
> Six million books.
> Give them a hunger for justice.

For Hesburgh, the project had taken on such significance that at
the age of 84 he traveled to Pedro Vicente Maldonado so he could
say Mass on the steps of AHD's first hospital the day it opened.

Still, that question: What made AHD a little engine that
could? For thousands of years humanity has been grappling with
an urgent need that seemed insoluble—how to regain the health
that was an ancestral birthright of the species. To better ourselves,

we had also worsened ourselves: We no longer wandered the face of the earth, instead setting ourselves up in villages where we gathered flocks of animals whose diseases we had no defenses against.

In the twentieth century, as health emerged again for some of the population, the idea arose that it must embrace every man, woman, and child—"Health for All." It's one of the freedoms we must have in order to be fully ourselves. On the eve of World War II, President Franklin D. Roosevelt recited his list of the four most basic freedoms: freedom of speech, freedom of worship, freedom from want, and freedom from fear. Two freedoms *to*, two freedoms *from*: freedoms to live life fully and freedoms from crippling burdens that diminish life. The right to health set forth five years later by Adrijia Štampar was a fusion, the freedom to enter a state that was "not merely the absence of disease and infirmity" guaranteed by the freedom from collapse into sickness and frailty.

Again: How had a small group like AHD been able to create health in ways that had eluded larger and more ambitious projects?

Before heading to Ecuador, I got a note from Mike Heisler, who'd worked for former president Jimmy Carter for seven years coordinating the Carter Center's river blindness program in sub-Saharan Africa. Heisler cautioned me that

when you come to Hospital Hesburgh, you won't necessarily see some of the big stuff going on in this organization. Traditionally small rural hospitals were not only not part of "Health for All" but, post–Alma Ata, they were absolutely not allowed at the table. Preventive care is great, but then you run into situations. I saw it myself in Kenya. People there would say, "Well, if you can't take care of my wife when she's having her baby, then I'm not interested in having a conversation with you." Small rural hospitals are redefining the "Health for All" agenda. In South America, David and Diego are one of the only games in town. Health care at this level— it impacts what has to be done in South Africa and South Asia as well. And guess what? In South Bend and South Dakota, too.

I wanted to see some of the "big stuff" not on display. David Gaus did some rummaging around at the hospital and at his hilltop home in Quito and turned over a whole stack of old papers. The standout document was a Xerox copy of a six-page, handwritten letter dated February 7, 1986, from a 23-year-old Gaus to "Dear Fr. Hesburgh," on the stationery of the Working Boys' Center in Quito. It had their slogan, *"una familia de familias"* (a family of families), and their logo, showing a small boy giving a man a shoeshine. Gaus's slightly backward-slanting cursive was tall and confident, and I realized it was the only thing I'd read by him that wasn't a medical paper.

At that point Gaus had been a live-in volunteer at the Working Boys' Center (WBC) for a year and a half. The center, since renamed the Working Families Center, is a nonprofit anti-poverty project set up in 1964 by Fr. John Halligan, a Jesuit from the South Bronx. Fr. Halligan had grown up knowing only that Ecuador had "Indians and jungles." He set up his program to help 100,000 school-age Quito boys, some no older than 5, who roamed the streets of the city from early morning till late at night, shining shoes, selling gum, and washing cars to help their families, many of which lived on less than two dollars a day.

Fr. John, called *padre* by the "shoeshine boys," started out serving free lunches in an attic, but by the time Gaus arrived in Quito, the WBC had its own building, served three meals a day, provided medical and dental care, taught trades and crafts, had after-school and sports programs, and enrolled whole families, not just boys, serving a hundred families at any given time. Every family had to open a savings account, and each family member— parents and sisters included—had to agree to finish grade school and then work for professional licenses as auto mechanics or carpenters or cosmetologists or in some other trade. The WBC day started with breakfast at 6:30 a.m.; at 8:00 the girls went to music class, and the boys went out to shine shoes. Everyone gathered for lunch, and there would be regular school classes in the afternoon, followed by dinner and games and chores. A 2007 analysis of the center concluded that with the program's help, five thousand Quito families had lifted themselves out of poverty.

Gaus's letter to Fr. Hesburgh is about joy, about poverty, and about Gaus's idea of what he should do with his life. It reads like a commentary on Fr. Hesburgh's favorite prayer, particularly the moment when a hunger for justice comes alive. The day-to-day life at the WBC was an altogether new experience for Gaus, as he told me on one of our drives: "Poverty—I never thought about it at all growing up. It's not something white middle-class kids in the Midwest even see. If we had to drive through a poor neighborhood we rolled up the windows."

Looking back now on his two years at the center, Gaus often refers to his "mid-life crisis at the age of 21," but in fact his questioning of things began in his junior year at Notre Dame, when his dad's sensible advice about becoming an accountant—"When a firm closes its doors and goes under, the last guy to be let go is the accountant"—no longer sounded like a rock to cling to. Even so, Gaus had enjoyed his freshman classes—at least up to a point. "I'd study for an hour or two," he said, "then play pool, shoot baskets, have a beer with a friend." Briefly he thought of joining the U. S. Air Force. After his disenchantment—"I wasn't a malcontent, just unhappy with my area of studies"—he found himself becoming "profoundly worried," asking again and again, "Why do I do what I do?"

A classmate of Gaus's, Lou Nanni, currently Notre Dame vice president for university relations, had written a paper on liberation theology and asked Gaus to read it. After that, Gaus said, "two nights a week, I'd call him at 11 p.m. and talk till 2." Nanni was going to Chile after graduation. Maybe, Gaus thought, Fr. Ted could help him get into the Peace Corps. Students knew that if you looked up at Hesburgh's office on the third floor of the old Main Building (where the Gold Dome is) or Hesburgh Library late at night and saw a light on—as was often the case—it was okay to climb up the fire escape and knock on the window. Which Gaus did. The Peace Corps idea didn't work out, but it opened another door—to a lifelong friendship. "I found out it's only a short hike up to the third floor."

Mike Heisler told me, "I used to think I was one of a few people Fr. Ted had put his arm around, and only later found out there are ten thousand of us. As with me and David, they all began with that lonely, late-night conversation."

Gaus's six-page letter (I'm abridging it somewhat) read:

Dear Fr. Hesburgh, Greetings once again from Quito, Ecuador. A lot has happened. I can begin by saying that I am very happy. I am so grateful to the Lord for giving me the courage to make the decision to come down here. I have had so many eye-opening experiences and have learned so much about David Gaus and my responses to what I have seen and experienced. And, more specifically, about the poverty. I moved from the initial shock of seeing it for the first time; to trying to convince myself that it really isn't a grave problem because nobody is dying in the streets of starvation; to simply not wanting to see it; and now to another point on the spectrum.

For about 6 months now I've been spending more time with families from the Center outside the Center on their "home court." It has opened my eyes to aspects of poverty that I never really considered before. I've grown especially close to one family, and although they constantly talk about how I've helped them, in no way does it compare to how they've helped me and taught me. What hurts me so much is that this whole poverty dilemma is no longer just a face or a photo or "those people down there." They are my *friends*! Although the pain and hurt are usually subtle, they are very real and constant.

I don't know where to go from here, to be perfectly honest with you. The walls of security that I had built in Milwaukee, Wis. and at Notre Dame are beginning to crumble and the realities of our world are becoming more visible. As I mentioned earlier, although this is a rough experience, I will be eternally grateful for it. I must respond—I must act. Not out of guilt, but out of love. Within the first few weeks after arriving here in Quito up until this very day, I have seen a problem that has caused a great deal of problems for these people: medical attention. Not only do they lack medical attention, but basic medical education as well. Something must be done about this. I am not a "save the world myself" type person, but I see this problem, and I feel as though I can make some difference. Even if it would be for a small community of people, I feel it would be worth it. A great deal of thinking has gone into this, and dialogue with many people. And as the day grows closer and closer for my return to the U.S.A. I also grow more and more convinced of this path. I'm capable of it, and I am going to do it. I want to be a doctor.

The letter goes on to say that Gaus would much prefer to return to Notre Dame for his pre-med work but assumes it will make financial sense to go home to Milwaukee, although, "I honestly don't know where to turn on this." He wonders if perhaps Fr. Ted might know of some scholarship money at Notre Dame so he could "contribute to the people on campus what I've seen and done and experienced here. Simply stated, I see it as a much better place to be than a state university. What can I say—I love the place."

What the letter doesn't say—what I pieced together from other accounts—was how much of a hit Gaus had made with the WBC families. There was no "rolling up of windows" in the way he approached things. "Kids loved him," a WBC graduate told me. "He played soccer with them and started a boxing club, and he taught English and social studies. Some of the American volunteers had the reputation of being too hard on the kids, but David was very caring and giving and would actually leave the center at the end of the day to walk the boys home. He'd come up with projects, while some of the other Americans were holed up in the office with coffee and cookies, keeping to themselves during their free time. For David it was never just digging weeds. He'd say, 'Let's plant a garden.' Literally. Someone found some seeds somewhere, and we had a harvest that year with huge pumpkins."

Gaus's letter says that he had "grown especially close to one family," but leaves it at that. This, I found out, was the Hinojosa family, and it was their story—a woman raising six sons and two daughters by herself on $100 a month—that had made such a profound impression on Gaus. Her husband, a policeman, left after the birth of their eighth child. For a while the Hinojosas lived on the northern edge of Quito in La Roldós, a newly settled area named for a populist president killed in a plane crash when he was only 40. La Roldós was a so-called "invasion neighborhood"—in the 1970s agrarian reformers had talked about expropriating derelict haciendas, but when no official action was taken, organized groups of fifty to a hundred people would arrive on a piece of land at six p.m. with tools and supplies and "settle" the area overnight, throwing up lean-tos and huts and fences, which made it difficult for police to respond once the sun came up. Sometimes the Hinojosa children had to take food and supplies up to their mother's small farm while bullets flew overhead. Eventually she got a deed to her plot in La Roldós, a huge thing for a poor woman in Ecuador. In the 1990s the area was officially incorporated into the city of Quito and got city services: electricity, drinking water, and sewers.

The Hinojosa residence Gaus got to know was a tiny house in a working-class neighborhood near the WBC that was actually an enormous abandoned adobe oven sitting on land that belonged to a relative. Gaus can still see the building in his mind's eye:

At first, I'd done what all self-respecting Germans do—you bury the image to keep the focus on the programs at the WBC. But the kids slept all piled up, all the brothers on a mattress on a dirt floor. There was a flimsy door, holes in the roof, and pigeons on the roof. I did what I could think of, built them a "Notre Dame bed"—a bunk bed. One of the boys had a chronic lung problem, maybe from sleeping on the floor. Then I noticed that other people who lived close by were in trouble, too. A pregnant woman didn't show up at the center one morning—she'd died in childbirth. Many of the "shoeshine boys" had scabies, a highly contagious skin disease that needs special drugs; it's caused by a burrowing mite, the "human itch mite," that produces small red bumps and blisters and a severe and relentless itch that's particularly bad at night. And they had head lice and were anemic. A WBC doctor told me that because of an iron deficiency they were also cognitively delayed—and their lives were already hard enough. There were people with TB and uncontrolled blood pressure who didn't take meds or even know they had it, and teenage pregnancies among 12- and 13-year-olds. It was not like being at a hospital and seeing rare and unusual conditions. These were people routinely encumbered by things I had never encountered.

Gaus has remained close to the Hinojosa family. All the boys are now responsible husbands and fathers: Five of them live in Quito; the sixth, along with one of the sisters and their mother, lives on the island of Minorca, in the Mediterranean. As for the second sister, Elizabeth . . . Gaus married her. They are raising three children, two daughters and a son.

Another person whose name didn't come up in the letter to Fr. Ted was Ronald H. Guderian, a young medical technologist and evangelical Protestant missionary at Vozandes ("Voice of the Andes") Hospital in Quito, a missionary hospital set up by a North American church group that also operated the only radio station in Ecuador that had even more listeners than Hólger Vesastiguí's Radio Zaracay. HCJB, short for Heralding Christ Jesus' Blessings, the first Christian missionary station in the world, went on the air in 1931. Gaus met Guderian one night when they were playing basketball in the Vozandes gym. His new acquaintance was researching tropical diseases. Specifically, he told Gaus, he had uncovered the presence of river blindness (onchocerciasis) in a community of the Chachi, an indigenous tribe in Ecuador's northwest coastal rainforest. It's a disease spread by black flies that breed along rivers, caused by a parasitic worm that moves from flies to people and can live within a human body as long as fourteen years, all that time producing a thousand larvae a day. If the disease goes untreated, these larvae, which can induce terrible itching, enter the eyes and can bring about permanent blindness.

Previously it had been assumed that river blindness occurred only in tropical Africa. Now it's thought that, as an unnoticed consequence of the "Columbian Exchange," it may have arrived in Ecuador on October 2, 1553, an otherwise joyous day when a slave ship bound for Peru foundered off the Ecuadorian coast—joyous because twenty-three slaves from Guinea escaped the wreck, declared their freedom, held off every attack by Spanish troops sent to subdue them, and became the nucleus of what is today a community of a million Afro-Ecuadorians.

Guderian said that finding river blindness had less impact than what happened right after, when he reported his findings to a Chachi chief. "Well," he remembered the chief's saying, "now that you've shown us we all have this infection and are going to go blind, what are you going to do about it? Leave us in this dome of gloom, or help us?"

"That question," Guderian told Gaus, "changed my life." He spent decades as one of the people working with Ecuadorian doctors and villagers to eradicate river blindness from the country—a task that finally became manageable with the Nobel Prize–winning discovery in Japan of an anti-parasite "wonder drug," ivermectin. Isolated from a soil-living bacterium, it's now considered as beneficial to humanity as penicillin or aspirin; it can be made into a pill that needs to be taken only once a year. In September 2014, WHO's director general officially confirmed that the worms that cause river blindness are no longer present anywhere in Ecuador.

Gaus's life began to change trajectory after his basketball game with Guderian. He told me:

> I got fascinated by parasites and how their life cycles intersected with our life cycles. It was our meeting in the hospital gym that sparked my interest in medicine. I'd seen a lot of people getting sick at the WBC. I wanted to keep giving back to the community, but the WBC work was short-term. I already knew I wanted to come back. Medicine seemed the ultimate way of being of service—and it was so intellectually stimulating, and it could be relevant, make a difference. That's how it started coming together. I would pray on it, chew on it. I loved doing service work, getting up at five, making breakfast, boxing classes at night; I'd go to bed exhausted but buzzing. I'd found a passion. But I needed a channel. I was doubting. Do I have the ability to carry through? I remembered people in my family saying, "You have to be smart to be a doctor." I knew I was excitable when I put my mind to something. I didn't yet know that finding something to be passionate about could give you endless energy and let you feel indefatigable. But it was true. When I began pre-med, I could sit down for four hours uninterrupted and walk away invigorated. And these weren't subjects—bio, chemistry— I'd ever considered interesting.

Gaus's brother, Danny, twelve years his junior, also spent a couple of years at the WBC and now lives in Ecuador, working in the flower export business. Danny was visiting Hospital Hesburgh during my stay there and told me he understood the kind of transformation David had gone through at the Center:

> We've a very provincial Midwestern family, we care about family and community, and we have the typical U.S. Irish-German immigrant background: pushed out of or escaping countries where earlier generations had seen grim events—

the Irish potato famine in the nineteenth century and the rise of Hitler in Germany after World War I. When Dave and I got to the Center—this was long before cell phones, and collect calls home were expensive, and letters were the only way to stay in touch—it felt like being at the end of the world. It opened my eyes to things Dave and I had never thought about, how without buying a ticket we happened to be born into a country that had won the global birth lottery, and how we'd never have been part of life in the U.S. if it hadn't been for earlier horrific events in Ireland and Germany.

Only one member of the family seemed to have a strong sense of this—my mom's dad, Herman Schmidt. He and Dave always had a great relationship, and as a boy Dave sat him down with a tape recorder and just riddled him with questions. Grandpa was a fascinating man with awesome memories—he'd studied to be a priest, fought in the German army in the First World War, and then, eyes already opened, deliberately shifted the circumstances of his life and by himself came to America. Later Grandpa told us, "If I'd stayed, I might've been put in charge of a concentration camp." Dave loved that Grandpa hadn't been afraid to take a risk. When Dave told Grandpa what he wanted to do with his life, there were tears of joy in Grandpa's eyes.

Several weeks after sending off his "Dear Fr. Hesburgh" letter, Gaus got a typed reply on the stationery of the Office of the President, University of Notre Dame:

Dear David: Your letter arrived as I was preparing to address our Junior Parents Weekend, and I read your letter to them as an example that we still have people like Dr. Tom Dooley [a special Notre Dame hero] coming to Notre Dame and graduating. Needless to say, I agree with all you say, and I'm delighted that you're going on to become a doctor. I am sure you can do it. I think you should come back to Notre Dame for your math and science. I know that will involve getting some help together on my part, but I will get it organized during the Summer.

The letter was signed, "Ever devotedly in Notre Dame, Father Ted."

CHAPTER SEVENTEEN

BEYOND THE
DOME OF GLOOM

FOR FATHER TED, "GETTING SOME HELP TOGETHER"
meant talking to his old friend Eppie Lederer, known to the read-
ers of 1,200 newspapers as the advice columnist Ann Landers.
Hesburgh had started including excerpts from Gaus's letter in
some of his speeches, including one at a college commencement
where he had shared the stage with Lederer. The two flew back to
Chicago together, and Lederer wanted to hear more about Gaus.
Hesburgh told her he was trying to come up with $20,000 for
Gaus's pre-med tuition for two years (Gaus's living expenses
would be covered if he became a resident assistant, or proctor, in
an undergrad dorm).

On the plane Lederer offered Hesburgh a check for the full
amount—but Hesburgh said no, he'd take only half now, and

they'd see how Gaus was doing after his first year. Gaus did more than well enough for Lederer to fund his second year. She then asked him about paying for med school; Gaus had already decided on Tulane, the only med school in the country offering a four-year M. D. and Master in Public Health and Tropical Medicine degree—which would cost $25,000 a year for tuition, room, and board.

Lederer handled this challenge adroitly. At a fundraising lunch for George H. W. Bush (Republicans hoped she'd become a supporter, despite being a lifelong Democrat), she kept talking about Gaus to a Bristol-Meyers executive she happened to be seated next to. He said the company didn't have scholarship programs, but she persisted—"Why can't you help this kid out?" Finally the man said, "OK, call my office Monday morning. Now let's get back to winning the White House!"

Dr. Thomas A. Dooley III, also mentioned in Fr. Ted's letter, was only 34 when he died in 1961. At the time he was the third-most-admired person in the United States (behind President Eisenhower and the Pope). In the early days of the Vietnam War, Dooley had established a thirty-five-bed hospital in a jungle village in nearby Laos, five miles from the Chinese border, where his patients called him "Thanh Mo America"—"Dr. America." Dooley had gone there because the country had only one "bonafide doctor" and because such a remote part of the world was the perfect place "to combat the two greatest evils afflicting it: disease and Communism."

There's a statue of Dooley near the Grotto on the Notre Dame campus; a miniature recreation of the famous shrine of healing at Lourdes, the Grotto had been a longtime dream of Fr. Sorin. Dooley is seen cradling a small boy in his left arm while a slightly larger girl on his other side gazes at him raptly. There's also a framed, stainless steel engraving of a letter Dooley wrote Fr. Hesburgh from a hospital bed in Hong Kong when, dying of cancer of the spine, he yearned for the nearness to God he had felt at the Grotto: "If I could go to the Grotto now I think I could sing inside."

Dooley's Laotian hospital didn't last—for all of Dooley's fame, it had functioned only through his repeated fundraising, and the day after his death it was overrun by Communist Laotian troops. What Gaus himself found inspirational about Dooley wasn't the heroic narrative that led the press to hail him as "The Splendid American," but something that was less talked about. Gaus said:

> Shortly after coming back to the States, I saw Tom Dooley's book, *The Edge of Tomorrow*. I found a quote from Albert Schweitzer, his talking about a "Fellowship of those who bear the Mark of Pain"—people for whom the suffering of others is something they must respond to. "Those who have learnt by experience what physical pain and bodily anguish mean, belong together the world over; they are united by a secret bond." Schweitzer went on, "He who has been delivered from pain, is now a 'man whose eyes are open.'"
>
> Sooner or later, Schweitzer thought, this duty to help would be universally recognized. But in the meantime he asked, "Whom shall we get to make a beginning?" A hundred years after Schweitzer posed the question, the idea *has* spread—witness the lives of Paul Farmer, or Carroll Behrhorst, or Scott Kellermann among the Batwa pygmies. The bond is no longer such a secret. Anyone who's endured a tragic illness or has lived through one that afflicted a family member or close friend is changed in a way that stays with you forever. Mike Heisler says that when you go to the most rural places in the world and see what happens to so many sick people there, as he and his wife have done, "You end up with clocks ticking in your head whenever you think of all the people not yet served."
>
> Here's something I jotted down when I heard it on National Public Radio a couple of years ago: "A new rite of passage is taking hold among ambitious young doctors—working the far corners of the poor world. The trend is striking. Of the new doctors coming out of U.S. medical schools in

the mid-80s, one in twenty had spent some real time abroad in health care. Ten years ago it was one in five. Last year, one in three." That's *me* they're talking about. All this was still rare in my day, the eighties. But it was practically unknown in Dooley's time, the forties, and almost unique in Schweitzer's, who got his medical degree in 1912. It's not just that the world has gotten smaller and getting to remote places has become easier. U. S. kids are more curious and less held in place by the post-Depression yearning for home, vacation cottage, car, and nice clothes—something we only recently started calling "the American dream," though the American dream has always been more far-reaching. They're looking for something they can be passionate about.

Anyway, when I read this in Dooley's book, it resonated. I had a small place within the Fellowship, the secret bond; it was an honor to join their ranks. And I was lucky—I'd found my passion. Looking at my letter to Father Ted thirty years later, I could see myself writing it, with the vision of what I wanted to do having just crystallized inside me. I understood that lack of health care is the ugliest manifestation of poverty. The elation I felt when he wrote back to me! Suddenly, a heavy hitter agreed with the plan I'd come up with. That he would take a chance on me, take a feeling I had and turn it into my life's mission, do something smart, effective, affordable, sustainable—for some of the poorest poor people on earth.

Then I thought, "Oh, my God, can I do this?" I was riddled with self-doubt. Back at Notre Dame that fall, the first chem quiz went okay, and the second chem quiz—I did well with that. Four weeks into the term came the first biology exam—a class of five hundred undergrads, and I was up against kids with two years of advanced placement bio in high school. They put printouts of campus I. D. numbers on a wall with test results. I walked over on pins and needles. My grade wasn't up there. I thought, "Oh, I did so poorly they didn't even post it." I went to Dr. Linda Margaret Hunt, the professor, who said, "Oh, yes, you're Gaus. Kind of a nontraditional student, aren't you? Haven't had biology in a while. Well, you got an 81, the third-highest grade in the class. Congratulations—clearly you're working hard and it's working out." I went back to my dorm, even a little tearful. Then I decided: There's no turning back. I was going to do it; I just had to work hard and be disciplined and it would happen. I might not be the brightest gem in the pile, but I had discovered my work ethic—*after* I'd found my passion.

John Breslin, a Notre Dame classmate of Gaus and now a lawyer, had a somewhat different take on his old friend "Gausser," whom he wrote about in sketches of his college days:

In 1981, when I met Dave, he was part of a group of roommates in Zahm Hall. I had just become a Zahmbie, and he was in the hallway. He had a quizzical smile that showed he was curious to meet me. He was wearing a short-sleeve plaid shirt, the kind you would picture young Ron Howard wearing in his Mayberry days. It was a paradigm of the all-American look, and he wore these shirts all the time—we called them Gausser shirts.

He was an accounting major who did not show a particular interest in that area, but it was evident early on that what made him tick more than anything else was other people. Whenever he was talking to someone, he would come to life. You would see the glimmer in his eyes, the hint of a smile. At some point it dawned on me that I knew several dozen people who considered Gaus as one of their three or four best friends. All of humanity is potentially in his immediate circle. You see, some are fascinated by music, some by money, some by football—but Gaus is one of those people who has such fun just being around people.

In Gaus's pile of papers, there was something he'd written about that time in his life:

I don't think I ever had an unhappy day in med school—neurology, pediatrics (though not so much general surgery, because there you're dealing with unhappy human beings). Most of life is grinding it out; you don't have too many of those epiphanous, if that's the word, life-changing days. But the years at Tulane were some of the best in my life, and I somehow even graduated fourth or fifth in my class. When I'd meet a cool prof I'd invite him over for dinner, get to know him, pick his brain, talk to him about everything from parasitology to politics. The school was a block from the French Quarter, and I met a lot of internationalists, fascinating people—many of the other public health students were already undersecretaries back in their own countries in Africa.

Gaus's mentor at Tulane, Dr. Barney Cline (a co-author of Gaus and Diego Herrera's WHO paper "Making Secondary Care a Primary Concern"), is a former president of the American Society of Tropical Medicine and Hygiene and also a longtime member of the AHD Advisory Board. He's a friendly man with a thoughtful, craggy, Spencer Tracy-ish look. The first time I met him, he brightened when I mentioned Gaus. He said:

The passion was always visible, from the day he got to Tulane. Back then I was chair of the joint degree in public health and tropical medicine. He came into my office, a big, handsome, strapping guy, and said, "Dr. Cline, I'm here because I'm going to Ecuador to start a clinic or found a hospital." No first-year med student had ever walked in to make that kind of declaration. I was skeptical, but he'd already put together his first team, which was him and a fellow med student and a Notre Dame grad who was working on a Ph.D. in international affairs, and they even had a name for themselves—Andean Health and Development. Their ideas weren't fully formed—well, how could they be? But David was always leaping ahead, already specifically thinking about work in the countryside. Needs were greater in remote areas. He thought if he stayed on at the Working Boys' Center, he'd wind up just taking care of routine aches and pains, a kind of on-call "doc in a box." He wanted to do something that would outgrow and outlive him.

I think, looking at the WBC and how much time Fr. Halligan had to spend fundraising, he wanted to come up with something that didn't depend on U. S. donors with open checkbooks. From the day he moved back to Ecuador, he coalesced a splendid group—part of it was Fr. Ted, but they all give of themselves. That's what's kept me involved. It started out very mom-and-pop-ish. I went to what was called a board meeting in Ecuador, just four or five people and Fr. Ted, who had a mischievous twinkle and some fine Cuban cigars he smuggled into the country. It was always Fr. Ted who wanted to know what was going to happen next, which is what he'd always done in his own life. To us he said, "This is God's work, even if it's all you ever do. But I think you can do more." And sometimes, "What's going on is great. Great. But when will you do something important?"

Dr. John F. Williams—"Skip" Williams, he's called—a former president of SUNY Downstate Medical Center in Brooklyn and himself a member of the AHD Advisory Board, told me that in med school you learn fifteen thousand new words and a new language. It got me thinking about David Gaus's days in med school—about what anyone goes through to get this training and why health seems so mysterious and elusive, even for those of us who won the global lottery, where robust health is the norm and expectation. Because even the long process of getting an M. D. takes you only so far. Evolution itself has made it difficult to wrap our minds around the subject. It isn't just that we avoid thinking about health—as we do, say, about death. It's that we're not really equipped to.

There's a recent book Barney Cline mentioned one day, *Understanding Pain: The Perception of Pain* by Fernando Cervero, a

Canadian doctor with a global perspective. Cervero was born in West Africa and educated in Spain; he has a Ph. D. as well as an M. D. He explained a technical part of this by making a distinction between the internal organs we can sense when they're not working properly and other organs we have no direct contact with.

Hollow organs, all of them connected to the world around us, such as the gallbladder, the bladder, or the gut, can send signals we experience as pain or discomfort. A heart attack is a powerful alarm, but most of the other solid organs, such as the liver, kidneys, spleen, or lungs, can't alert us to their state or even their location. They simply have no links we can bring into awareness, even when a doctor asks, "Where does it hurt?"

The polite question when you run into someone is about his or her health—"How are you?" But there's a lot about the question that's unanswerable. Occasionally we notice our heartbeat or our breathing, and we can move awkwardly or with precision and feel a few bones here and there, but we're so blind and deaf to our insides that they can seem as oddly unknown, as far away and unreachable, as the center of the earth.

Some doctors, like Gaus and Diego Herrera, emerge from med school having mastered the fifteen thousand new words and able to visualize what's inside, but with their sense of unknowingness and unknowableness intact. This awareness of how finite new knowledge is has a more general name: humility. Put another way, humility makes a good companion for anyone joining the Fellowship of Pain, which itself has a more familiar name—empathy.

About all this, Gaus said:

When I finished all my training—pre-med at Notre Dame, Tulane, family medicine residency at the University of Wisconsin—and returned to Ecuador, that's when my education began. I started to learn. And there was so much to learn—how to listen, how to partner with other doctors and patients, how long everything takes, even how long *learning* takes! And with so many bumps along the way. At one point or another, we've probably made every mistake you can think of. But maybe that's how we got stronger. "We make the road by walking," the Brazilian educator, Paulo Freire, used to say, echoing the great Spanish poet, Antonio Machado, *"Se hace camino al andar. Al andar se hace camino"*—"The road is made as you march. As you move on, paths appear." Words I first heard applied to Carroll Behrhorst. Better knowledge, when it comes, can affect people's lives. That's the thrill, the rush.

CHAPTER EIGHTEEN

IN AN
ECUADORIAN WAY

AFTER HIS RESIDENCY, GAUS "PRE-POSITIONED" HIMSELF for Ecuador by training residents at the same Milwaukee hospital, St. Luke's, where he'd just been a resident (it's now the Aurora St. Luke's Medical Center). This helped him make money for living expenses in Ecuador and also set up what later became his three-thousand-mile "commute" between Ecuador and the States, doing summertime family medicine stints and ten-hours-a-day shifts in the St. Luke's emergency room. "I couldn't very well open a private practice in Milwaukee that would only be open two months a year," he said. "This was also my yearly continuing medical ed program, working in a place where around every corner there's a cardiologist, a kidney doctor, a pulmonologist, an infectious disease doctor—I'd corner these guys and say, 'What's new in heart failure?' 'What are the new meds?' They were great ten-minute cram sessions."

In the summer of 1997, a dozen years after writing his "Dear Fr. Hesburgh" letter, Dr. David Gaus returned to Ecuador with his wife and their first child. "Thanks to Ann Landers and Bristol-Meyers," Gaus told me, "I came down here debt-free and could live on a shoestring for five years." In addition, Gaus and one of his original AHD Tulane partners, Erik Janowsky, had secured a $40,000 start-up grant from CARE International and USAID, enough to open the small primary health care center they'd set their hearts on back in med school and during their public health training—a two-room outpatient storefront clinic on a back street in the countryside town of Pedro Vicente Maldonado. Their partner in this project, a local physician, lived upstairs in an apartment with his family. It all happened rather quickly, in about six months, and pretty much according to expectations.

"So it was actually twelve years after I mailed my letter," Gaus said, "that my intensive learning began. The learning I hadn't known I needed." The day of that conversation, Gaus and I were taking a side trip from Santo, where Gaus now spends most of his time, to Pedro, so we could see the hospital he never expected to build; it's down the street from where the storefront clinic was. It's a gleaming, beckoning, sun-drenched yellow, by far the most colorful building in town. To keep it glowing, it gets repainted every two years with constant in-between touch-ups.

Gaus and I were sitting in stackable plastic lawn chairs on the open-air, second-floor balcony of Hospital Pedro Vicente Maldonado, drinking Inca Kola, a carbonated, extremely sweet Peruvian cream soda that's said to taste like "liquid bubblegum"—it's an even more intense and lemon-colored yellow than the hospital walls. The balcony is by far the best place in town to wait out an approaching thunderstorm. It looks out over low flat roofs, clotheslines, and green ridges to beyond the edge of town, which is always quite close by, no matter where you are; the floor has alternating squares of concrete and free-form white, aquamarine, and slate-gray mosaic tiles. There's always a faint breeze at least, and when the rain comes, it rumbles comfortably on the parabolic plastic roof.

Gaus said:

> Maybe the best thing you can say about those years of preparation in the States was that they showed me how unprepared I was. Dripping wet behind the ears when I arrived, though the best decision Erik and I made was going to the countryside. It's still where the need is greatest, where poverty is the most persistent. President Correa once told reporters that the Bible got things right when it talked about plenty alternating with famine, in Pharaoh's dream of seven fat cows followed by seven thin cows. But in Ecuador, he said, despite great changes, "We are always in the area of thin cows."
>
> I knew I wanted to go to a tropical or subtropical area—since I was already interested in tropical diseases. The summer before I graduated from Tulane, I got an internship in Ecuador with the river blindness program and worked over in the dome of gloom with a surgeon carving parasites out of people. In 1997, Elizabeth and I and our little daughter, Gabriella, moved to Quito. Already I was determined to commute from there to wherever I'd be working, so that the gringo doctor wasn't the face of the organization—it had to be Ecuadorian-driven. If the hospital were thought of as a "gringo place," then we'd have a harder time convincing people that "we did this ourselves—and for ourselves."
>
> The decision to work at one remove was a departure from the Carroll Behrhorst model. It's unusual for an outsider to be an invisible catalyst. But we're not a flash in the pan, and we're not a traveling circus, here for a couple of days and then gone. Instead we're building a relationship with the community, a continuity. Of course, not living nearby meant I was out of touch whenever I went home, since back then the only person in our Quito neighborhood who had a phone knew someone who knew someone who knew the president.

There was one spot in the kitchen where sometimes I could stand and make a call on a wireless phone.

But where could we set up shop? If I went east, down the Andes to the Amazon region, it would take too long to get there. If I went west on the southerly route, that went through Santo Domingo, and I swore I'd never go to Santo! It was such a big morass. So we wound up in PVM, which was west of Quito but on the northerly route.

We were so sure our little storefront clinic held the keys to the kingdom—selective primary health care, oral rehydration, immunization, and family spacing, a polite term for birth control. In our two rooms, each about ten feet by twenty feet, we had antibiotics, an exam table, a delivery bed, a desk, a stainless steel table with some surgical instruments, a glass stand with medications and injectables. What more did we need?

Then, as I told you, the lightning bolts struck, showing us our helplessness—we might as well be out in the Gobi Desert. Alfredo, the 7-year-old boy who got bitten by the *equis*, the kid who told me, *"Doc, voy a morir"*—"Doc, I'm going to die." Roberto, the 9-year-old whose right leg had become a piece of dry charcoal after he was mistreated for an *equis* bite. The young father-to-be whose wife died at home from a preeclampsia seizure and who could only tell us, "She fell asleep. Can you fix her?" The people and things you never forget. The grim understanding of what happened to people we couldn't help and had to send off to Quito. Like Isabel, 17 years old, with acute appendicitis, and 43-year-old Gustavo, with a broken femur, ironically the longest, strongest bone in the body, both of whom died on the way to Quito because, well, we couldn't operate on Isabel and we couldn't set Gustavo's bone properly.

Not that getting all the way to Quito meant help was guaranteed. José, a 40-year-old farmer, was brought to us one afternoon in the back of a jolting, bouncing pickup truck. He couldn't move his legs or even feel them. He and a helper had been chopping down trees when a large branch fell on his back, knocking him to the ground. When he couldn't get up, his helper ran away. When he didn't come home for lunch, his wife went looking for him and heard his screams. There was no choice—his breathing was worsening, and I had to use the same pickup truck to have him transferred that night to Quito. Unlike the young farm worker I once had to ship off to Quito with acute pesticide poisoning and who died there, unattended, in a hospital emergency room hallway, José survived but was paralyzed for life. I still think his ride to the capital in the back of that pickup truck actually worsened his spinal cord injury.

Clearly, Pedro Vicente Maldonado needed a hospital. We'd been told that, even before the lightning bolts. We hadn't listened. Erik had been in Ecuador a few months before I got there and conducted a survey of the townspeople, a feasibility study with some USAID money. They said they wanted a hospital and would pay for its services although they couldn't pay as much as people in Quito did. But we were tone-deaf, locked into our preconceptions, thinking they just didn't understand their real needs.

Meanwhile they didn't know how to listen to us, either. This, too, was our fault. I realized then I had to become tri-cultural—know how to think like people in Milwaukee, like people in Quito, and like people in Pedro.

For instance, I could see that 70 percent of all the women and children in Pedro were iron deficient. Now, the best way to get iron is to eat meat. Beef is best, though pork, itself a rich iron source, is just as widely available. But in the Ecuadorian countryside, when people get a bruise from a fall or a cut from a machete, they're always told, "Don't eat pork—it'll make it infected." I'm not sure where this comes from; it's not exactly Biblical. They have nothing against eating pigs as a rule. They eat guinea pigs, for that matter, *cuy* as they call them, native to the Andes and the main source of protein before cattle were introduced. But no pork after a cut. I think I spent five years reassuring people, saying, "You know what? Don't worry about this pork thing." They would kind of look at me funny. After a while I stopped mentioning pork, and finally I started saying, "Hey! Make sure you don't eat any pork because you might get a secondary infection." Then people said, "Eh, the gringo's finally learned something. Now I believe this guy."

I couldn't help asking Gaus if they were eating pork now.

"No," he said. "But they're actually coming to see us for other stuff. Which is a much better outcome."

I reached for another Inca Kola (two definitely being my limit). Gaus, after three, had already had enough. He said:

Hospital Pedro Vicente Maldonado was officially inaugurated in March 2001, several years after my belated epiphany. The total price tag was $960,000. I love being able to say we built and equipped a hospital for less than a million dollars, especially since in the States a teaching hospital now costs a million and a half *per bed*.

We still had an outpatient clinic, considerably expanded, and under the same roof a seventeen-bed hospital for those who needed surgery or recuperation time after an illness or injury. And an operating room, a labor and delivery suite, an emergency room with five cubicles, a diagnostic lab so we could run our own tests, an X-ray machine, and upstairs an auditorium/kitchen. As of now, there's a staff of fifty—twenty-five care providers, fifteen administrators, and ten more to handle maintenance, cleaning, cooking, and laundry. All Ecuadorians, taking care of 25,000 patients a year. Which breaks down to two thousand outpatients and more than a hundred hospitalizations every month. HPVM is the biggest employer in town, and it's become prestigious to work there. By now a third of the people in town have been there, which means someone in everyone's family or someone they know.

From the start we had several goals. To provide high-quality health care twenty-four hours a day, seven days a week, for a population with very few resources. To turn no one away. To make the facility self-sustaining so it wouldn't be just another missionary hospital kept afloat by outsiders. And to do this in an Ecuadorian way, which meant the longevity of the operation would be the key to its success. We already knew you can't just go into a community for a year and expect to make a difference.

In an Ecuadorian way.

There's an AHD video of the first woman, Digna Ramirez, to give birth at the hospital rather than at home—a healthy boy; they were discharged the next day. Digna Ramirez talks about how uncertain she was beforehand: "Sometimes the mother or the child dies, but if you trust in doctors, they know more." Gaus remembers her doubts about whether to come to the hospital in the first place and whether to spend the night—since everyone knew that hospitals were places to die.

Somehow I was even more impressed by what I heard the next day from Theresa, the *dueña*, or owner, of Panadería Migue, a very small corner bakery on Pedro Vicente Maldonado's Central Park, the town's small paved public plaza, a short walk from the hospital. Tiny as it is, you get the feeling that whatever happens in Pedro filters through Migue (a nickname for Miguel) without delay, which is perhaps why Gaus wanted me to meet Theresa.

We sat on three plastic stools under posters for Coke, Nestlé Huesitos ("little bones," a calcium-fortified kids' drink), and Pony Energía (a caramel-flavored nonalcoholic beer from Colombia that's a regional favorite), and ate just-baked *pan dulce de Ecuador*, sweet, pillowy rolls that are golden brown on top. We said hello to Theresa's gray-eyed granddaughter, who'd just been given a full scholarship to a university in Quito and was planning to study international relations and travel to France and Turkey. A gray striped cat with light green eyes wandered through our legs.

Theresa, an energetic woman with short-cropped hair and wearing a bright pink shirt, was herself one of HPVM's early patients. Her late husband, an important person in Pedro who donated land for a local school and a cemetery, and her daughter-in-law have also been treated there. When I asked Theresa about the hospital, she shrugged. "Well, we still use it, of course. It was exciting initially, and now we've settled into it. It's become the background to our lives."

Strolling back to the hospital, Gaus said he was thrilled to hear that—far better, he said, to be part of people's lives than to be universally adored. He saw it as a turning point, when a community moves beyond gratitude. "By the way," he said, "the best part is it's not a typical Schweitzer or Tom Dooley–style hospital dependent on its founders. It runs better now than when I was there every day."

CHAPTER NINETEEN

HOW TO *BE*
A HOSPITAL

GAUS MAKES LIGHT OF IT THESE DAYS—THE PHYSICAL,
visible part of setting up a hospital—finding land, designing,
building, and equipping the structure, and paying for everything.
"Yeah, we needed some working capital to get going," he recently
told a lunch crowd at the Notre Dame Club in Chicago. "But
now we don't need a *centavo.*"

When he was living through it, though, the project often felt
close to foundering. Things started off well—the town offered
some of the construction costs and a long, skinny plot of land (the
hospital, as a result, is itself somewhat long and skinny). Thanks
to Fr. Hesburgh, the country's then–finance minister, who had an
M. A. and a Ph. D. from Notre Dame, promised a $200,000 con-
tribution. But some of the town's ways of doing business created
difficulties. The mayor, at first a staunch AHD friend, came up

for re-election, and some money Gaus thought had been ear-marked for the hospital got spent buying tires for county cars and trucks and for painting the school—pre-election moves that upset so many people that the mayor was defeated. The hospital stayed neutral in the fight, but once out of office the former mayor and his patron, the local parish priest (the mayor had once been the priest's chauffeur), spread rumors alleging that Gaus was going to sell the hospital to developers of a strip mall and return to the United States with a million dollars in his pocket.

It was Diego Herrera who quietly pointed out that the hospital had become popular, so all the priest had to do was say he'd always been its champion, never mind what had gone on before. Herrera saw that this would, as he said, *llevar la fiesta en paz*—keep the party going peacefully.

Herrera had a remarkable range of abilities, seemingly from birth. He'd grown up in a small mountain town fifty miles south of Quito, part of a family of community leaders and politicians, many of whom, Gaus discovered, had "a great nose for political strategy." A great-uncle on his mother's side had been president of Ecuador. Herrera is somewhat shy and a voracious reader—he studied anthropology and sociology, has an M. A. in the methods and practices of teaching, and his heroes are Washington, Jefferson, Martin Luther King Jr., and Gandhi "because they changed their social circumstances."

Herrera landed in Pedro because, after med school in Quito, he'd taken the highly unusual step—in Ecuador—of completing a family medicine residency. That way, he said, he could become "a real doctor." He told Gaus at the time, "I don't want to be a dumb mule making a lot of money."

"Just make sure you keep him busy," Gaus had been told when he met Herrera for the first time. "He gets bored."

"Well," Gaus says now, "I worked him to the bone. He saw fifty patients a day. I was thoroughly impressed, but I burned him out. He only spent a year with us then, and for three years he went to an international aid group trying to get health projects started and picked up a lot of administrative experience. But he found himself disillusioned, saying, 'We had giant budgets and stayed on the top floors of hotels eating lobster and talking about poverty. But we didn't build any hospitals.'"

So Herrera returned to Hospital Pedro Vicente Maldonado, this time as hospital administrator and just in time to solve another crisis. A financial one. HPVM was up and running, still popular with the town and drawing patients from a swath of countryside that stretched for a dozen miles in one direction and fifty in another and was home to seventy people. But HPVM was having trouble covering its operating expenses.

As Gaus tells the story:

The hospital was functioning the same way rural Ecuadorian communities function—in a constant state of financial crisis. You could fall flat on your face any day. We were as close to the edge as a single mom with six kids and four cows. Everyone could stay fed—unless one of the kids got so sick that the mom would have to take him to Quito, in which case she might lose the cows while she was away and everyone would go hungry.

Diego's first stroke of genius came with the suppliers who were pounding down the door, looking for payment. Money we'd earned and would get but hadn't come in yet. Diego decided it was easier to pay the small accounts and leave one or two big ones, because a couple of phone calls a day were better than two dozen. Then, after ignoring some of the calls from a big supplier, he told the man, "I'll pay $5,000 a month for four months, starting next week"—we didn't even have $5,000 on hand—"but I need $2,000 worth of medications in two days because my shelves are empty. How can I pay you if I don't continue to sell?" The man never filled the order, but a week later, when he called to pick up the first check for $5,000, Diego exploded: "I thought we had an understanding! You gave me your word about that delivery. I can't trust you anymore. Our deal is off. Now I don't know when I'll be able to pay you. I'm bitterly disappointed. Call me in three months if you're ready to be forthright." And then he slammed down the phone. Three months later we had the money and Diego had successfully pulled off the stall.

Money problems had been far worse in the early days, when the hospital was in its planning stages and then under construction. Erik Janowsky had gone back to the United States to work on his Ph.D., which meant that Gaus and his original local partner had to run the existing Pedro clinic 24/7 by themselves while also thinking about the new hospital. Gaus was burning through the money he had made from his work in Milwaukee, and his second child—a son, Christopher—was born prematurely and had to spend a month in a neo-natal ICU in Quito. (He's fine, now.) Gaus maxed out his credit cards and owed $26,000. He remembers one bleak night, thinking, "What the hell am I doing here?" He still gets shivers remembering that time, a period when he thought he was doing well if he "had one or two good days a month."

In the summer of 1999, with a design in hand and ground already broken for the hospital, Gaus needed another $200,000 "or we were dead in the water." Gaus took the family back to Milwaukee on a trip for his usual summer stints at St. Luke's Hospital. He spoke to his father's brother, a banker, and they came up with the idea of getting some local Notre Dame alumni interested in supporting the hospital. A couple of days later, a man his uncle knew, a partner with one of the big public accounting firms, wrote Gaus a check for $2,000 on the spot and said, "Now, David, that wasn't so hard, was it? You've already convinced me. Let's invite a bunch of Domers to lunch at the Wisconsin Club"— "Domers" being Notre Damers; the reference is to the Golden Dome of the Main Building. The Wisconsin Club, originally the Deutscher Club, Milwaukee's most distinguished private club, is housed in a gargantuan, ornate mansion downtown that's the same age as the Dome itself.

On a second visit to the Panadería Migue—the pan dulce is worth a second visit—Gaus relived that long-ago lunch:

There were a bunch of helpful people there, but the two most important guys were Dan Meehan, an Irishman from New York who'd started life as a longshoreman but now owned a shipping company in the Port of Milwaukee, and Mike Hansen, like me a Notre Dame accounting major—he'd also worked for the same accounting firm as our luncheon host, but fifteen years earlier left to buy a school-bus company that he turned into a gigantic regional school-bus system in southeast Wisconsin. An unpretentious, unassuming, wonderful person who lived in my parents' neighborhood. We've become close, close friends—I've been to all his kids' weddings, and he's always there to help me think things through.

I can attest to this, having sat through a conference call in Madison, Wisconsin, some months later. Gaus, in the company of the entire AHD support staff, spent several hours on the phone in an intense conversation about Hospital Hesburgh's budget projections with Hansen, who was in Florida. We were in Madison because, starting in 2010, Gaus had become a part-time clinical professor of medicine at the University of Wisconsin, where he was in charge of family medicine residents and also taught global health to undergrads.

Befitting a bare-bones nonprofit, the entire paid AHD support staff consists of one person, Laura Dries. (Previously, Gaus's sister, Susan, had handled office chores on a volunteer basis out of her home in New London, Wisconsin, while his dad, in Milwaukee, had been the unpaid bookkeeper.)

Boundlessly energetic and seemingly unflappable, with an M.B.A./M.A. in Latin American Studies, Laura Dries took the job in 2009, when Hansen urged her to apply. "As of now, all my work is remote," she says, since every day, working out of a one-room office, she's either exchanging emails with Diego Herrera in Ecuador or on the phone with AHD board members (the board is bigger now, having signed up some of Gaus's fellow Domers, Class of 1984). Or doing both at once.

"It's a team," Mike Heisler says, "a bi-national team. That's what's unique about AHD, and I say this after working on desperate situations in sub-Saharan African countries, both English- and French-speaking. We're a family able to stretch ties across a hemisphere. In fifteen years there hasn't been a single day I didn't wake up and think about Ecuador, even when I was teaching and doing hospital work in Atlanta or running a six-state telemedicine ICU program across the Great Plains while in Sioux Falls, South Dakota."

Gaus took up the 1999 lunch story again:

Mike Hansen immediately said he wanted to join the AHD board. On many, many late nights he was the guy on the other end of the phone when I'd call to say, "$15,000 payroll due tomorrow." Somehow a fix always turned up, and he'd say that his wife always said that the hand of the Lord is on my shoulders.

Sometimes I think there are three things that keep me going—my commitment to the people in Ecuador; my commitment to Fr. Ted; and my commitment to Mike Hansen. So, halfway through that lunch, who should walk in but Dan Meehan, who told everyone he'd just come from loading a container of donated medical supplies from some belly-up clinic in Milwaukee, and he was shipping it off to South Africa. In addition to owning a shipping company and a foundation that supports charitable medical projects all over the world, Dan is also a Knight of Malta, part of a Catholic organization that dates back to the Crusades—when it was set up to defend Jerusalem. Today their mission is to promote health care in 120 countries, and they're considered a sovereign nation under international law, so when Dan ships off containers full of hospital beds and X-ray machines, the local customs people can't open the back doors, which prevents a huge amount of pilferage.

Dan comes in sweaty and grungy, but he sits down and listens to me for about fifteen minutes. Then he says, "How much money do you need?" I said $150,000. He said, "I'll give it to you. Come over to my house tomorrow and we'll work out the details." After lunch, I got back in my car and started crying. Dan had literally put us on the map. Elizabeth saw my red eyes when I got home and thought something bad had happened. I told her about Dan's gift and cried some more. I think the year and a half up to that point had just caught up with me.

By the time HPVM opened it doors—this was after another year and a half, in March 2001—the total U.S. contribution had grown to $600,000. Half of that was cash, and half in donated medical equipment from Dan Meehan. With Fr. Ted's help, we got Saludesa's nonprofit status officially approved. ["Saludesa"—a play on *salud*, the Spanish word for health—is the Ecuadorian name for Andean Health and Development.] He met with Gustavo Noboa, then the Ecuadorian president, when he came down for the hospital inauguration. At Carondelet Palace, the Ecuadorian White House, Fr. Ted humbly pleaded our case as an important national project.

I only heard later, from one of the board members who came down for the opening, that Fr. Ted was privately still skeptical about whether "the kid could pull it off" and make the place sustainable. He was willing to back me but not ready to pronounce a victory. Also while in Ecuador, Fr. Ted had to straighten something else out. *Me.* I'd been spending so much time at the hospital, Elizabeth was basically a single parent. He took me aside and said that if an old priest like him could say Mass every day of his life—the accomplishment he was most proud of, by the way—then I could figure out how to get home every night for dinner. It was a matter, he said, of learning how to excuse myself for "another important meeting"—with my family, of course, though only I needed to know that. Then he gave us all his blessing.

Gaus and I took a slow walk back to the hospital. Pedro looks slightly more "townish" when seen lengthwise—the main street, which runs along the crest of a low ridge, is about fifteen blocks long. When you look crosswise at street corners, you're always looking downhill, and fields and trees are only a couple of blocks distant in either direction. It was a sleepy afternoon, the air somewhat fresher and cooler than before; a thunderstorm had come and gone while we were at the *panadería* (bakery). A couple of small boys were flipping poker chips on the shelf of a closed market stall, and a couple of older boys were kicking around a soccer ball.

Gaus said:

So far you and I have been talking about how to build a hospital. But we had to learn how to *be* a hospital, something most doctors never find out how to do—and certainly not most U.S. doctors because they stay in private practice. The list of things you need to know goes on and on. Some of it's just practical, like what to do if the electricity goes out and there's no water. Well, you have to have a generator and surge protectors, and that way you know several key pieces of equipment won't break down—your EKG machine, your anesthesia machine, and your pulse oximeter, which measures how much oxygen reaches someone's extremities with each heartbeat, something you need in an operating or recovery room. For an uninterrupted supply of water, you build a cistern and buy a tanker, and periodically refill the cistern at five dollars a load. We also treat all our water. Then there's the question of how clean is clean enough? The first people we hired assumed that hospital clean was the same as household clean, which basically meant no garbage on the floor. That wasn't good enough, of course.

A lot was administrative and had to do with finding the right people. Is my accountant robbing me? I need to trust him with the $70,000 purchase of an ambulance, and I wouldn't trust him with a $300 bicycle. What do you do about doctors who don't show up in the ER for surgery or nurses who quit at a moment's notice? What quantities of medicines do you need to keep on hand? You develop a "minimum stock trigger" that tells you when to reorder oxygen or atropine, which we need for acute toxic reactions to spraying organophosphate pesticides without protective clothing. That's when a farmer comes in displaying signs of "SLUDGE syndrome," which stands for involuntary salivation, lacrimation (crying), urination, diaphoresis (sweating), gastrointestinal upset (diarrhea), and emesis (vomiting). You have to act fast. Atropine has brought a lot of people back from the brink of death.

We had to institutionalize the place—make sure, for instance, that the head nurse knew how to evaluate everyone's strengths and weaknesses in staff meetings and how to give her own opinion. Our problem was that the first guy running the meetings, a typical macho guy, would cut the nurse off whenever she started to talk. When discussions did start, they would quickly shift to something else—they'd start joking about what they had for dinner—and then the meeting was over. Now the meetings run efficiently and no one cuts anybody off.

Elizabeth helped us find the cheerful yellow for the main outpatient waiting room and the exam rooms, and she was particularly good at working with the shy young women in Pedro, high school students we hired as receptionists.

Elizabeth had come to the States to marry Gaus when he was still a medical student, and later she got a degree in bilingual elementary ed in Milwaukee, planning on teaching in Ecuador. But once they were back in the country, it turned out that Gaus needed her help getting HPVM ready to open its doors.

When I asked Elizabeth how she drew out the young women in Pedro, she said she made a point of asking the trainees about their own experiences at a hospital or clinic, what they hadn't liked or would've liked, did they feel ignored, and so on, and from there they practiced saying hello and good morning and making everyone feel especially welcome. Elizabeth told me, "I had to remind them, 'You need to smile' and 'You have such a beautiful smile. What does it take to get you to smile?' David built this hospital for poor people, but when it opened it was so light and fresh they couldn't believe it was okay for them to be there or that it was a hospital. They would wipe off their shoes when they came inside. We had to reassure them this place was for them."

CHAPTER TWENTY

AN UNREMARKABLE
ROOM

HOSPITAL PEDRO VICENTE MALDONADO LOOKS MUCH today as it did when it opened—it's antiseptically clean, the receptionists smile in the main waiting room, which is the same cheerful yellow and now full of families (fifty people turn up by 8:00 a.m.). There's a big picture window looking out onto the street, part of the original design. What's new is a large flatscreen TV on one wall that shows hi-def nature videos and the same sleek, comfortable metal-mesh chairs as the ones at Hospital Hesburgh.

The cheerfulness extends to the exam rooms (*consultorios*), where three walls are painted two shades of yellow, while the fourth wall has two shades of light blue. Each room has a large window; the floor tiles are white and forest green. A polished stone counter has a sink for scrubbing up at one end and a computer at the other, for displaying X-rays and test results. In the brightly lighted wards in the back, blankets have the Saludesa crest—a snow-capped Andean peak with a content-looking family. The nurse's station has several empty clipboards formerly used for handwritten records, saved now as museum pieces, relics of HPVM's pre-paperless past.

Adriana Quishpe, the director of administrative operations, is herself a former HPVM receptionist who's lived her whole life in Pedro and went to grade school and high school there. While already at the hospital, she went to night school for college and put herself through a remote-learning M. A. program in management so she could create what became the records system that's used today. "I want everyone who comes here to feel this is their home," she said when she met me.

Gaus and I went upstairs to a wood-paneled area with an informal, chalet-like feel and a long table for early-morning conferences. He said:

> The front door to the hospital was the interface between world views. The community needed to know how to use a hospital. Let's say a man is admitted with blood pressure of 70/40 after a gunshot wound. Normal blood pressure is 120/80, and anything below 90/60 means you're in danger of not getting enough oxygen and nutrients to your organs. Essentially, you can't remain alive with a reading of 70/40.
>
> But if you don't die until after you reach the hospital, then people want to know, what did *they*—the doctors—do wrong? Or an elderly couple comes in. The wife has something, but she won't sit across from me and never meets my eyes. It sounds like machismo on my part, but unless I get buy-in from the husband, she can't be helped. You're not going to change the way a couple thinks during ten minutes in an exam room. Let's say you want her to come back for a follow-up. Some people are convinced that injectable medicine works better than pills even when the injection won't do much good or the pills are equally good. So if you agree up

front to give them a shot, it's likely they'll do the follow-up. An injection is the candy you offer.

So much of this I learned from Diego. How did Diego learn? Gradually. Doing, doing wrong, correcting, modifying. Watching Diego with people—that was far and away most important. It comes up even more strongly in Santo if we're treating someone from the Tsáchila community. A man with a fever, say, which might be dengue or malaria. If you value that man's world view—his *cosmovisión*, in Spanish, his *Weltanschauung*, if you'd rather—then there's more chance he'll validate yours. He believes that a *curandero* takes fever darts out of people and directs them at other *curanderos*, who have a protective shield around them, and that people can fall ill if the darts bounce off that other shaman's shield and hit them instead. So my first question will be "Where do you think the arrow got you?" "I got hit right here," he'll say. Which tells me where he's hurting. I'll ask how close he lives to the *curandero*—a hundred feet? Two hundred? Because maybe that's a factor. Then if I give him antibiotics and tell him they'll help with the fever, too, he's likely to take them.

Here in Pedro, early on we came to an understanding with some of the local masseuses, a big part of the town's *camino a la cura*—because people in farming communities fall out of trees or tumble off houses raised up on stilts so snakes can't get in. They get banged up, and a massage can work out some of the aches and pains. Sometimes the masseuse may suspect a fracture, something a rub-down can't fix.

We had a local kid named Carlos Alvarado who was our X-ray tech. He was good. We even sent him to Quito for a two-week course sponsored by the Atomic Energy Commission to learn the theoretical concepts of radiation therapy. So the masseuses found out that someone from the community was running this machine that could see inside your body, and they started sending him their suspicious fractures, and he would check the X-rays with one of our doctors to see if there was a broken bone but would report back to the masseuses under his own name. At which point they started sending the actual fracture cases to us directly. Which worked out for everyone. People got well and didn't have problems from bones that hadn't healed properly—and nobody had forced a different point of view or *cosmovisión* on anyone else.

On the drive back to Santo, Gaus said, "Now I can tell you my 'secret sauce' story"—how the hospital found an Ecuadorian way to become self-sufficient and set itself apart from missionary hospitals dependent on outside cash." It was one thing, Gaus said, for AHD to have raised money to build HPVM, but now it needed to cover its operating expenses while at the same time turning no one away.

Not that the hospital's charges were exorbitant—quite the contrary. A blood test was $2, an office visit $3, and a C-section or surgery for appendicitis cost under $200. The problem was that, even so, only a third of the people in and around Pedro, whose income averaged $150 a month, could afford these prices. It took years to come up with the answer. A number of strategies were tried, with limited success, and then the solution fell into their laps.

First, it occurred to Gaus to revisit his long-neglected accounting skills. "I started peeling off the cobwebs and using terms I hadn't spoken since undergrad days," he told an interviewer from the Notre Dame business college. "The synapses started firing again." At 5:00 a.m. during one of his stints in Milwaukee, he began calculating fixed costs and pharmacy and lab costs. He got an idea—AHD could sell health insurance to people in Pedro for $30 per adult per year and $15 for each child.

But in rural Ecuador twenty years ago this turned out to be one of those areas in which world views were not easily reconciled. Someone would turn up with acute appendicitis, buy a $30 package, put $10 down, get the surgery, go home, and never send the second payment. Or someone else would say at the end of a year, "Doc, we never used the service, we didn't get sick. So we get our money back, right?" The model worked better with large groups; a union that represented the workers of a provincial government signed up five hundred members. Six months later, though, the payments stopped arriving, and it turned out that the charismatic union president, also the lead singer in one of the most popular salsa orchestras in the country, had gone underground and for the past six months had been sleeping in the backseats of different cars.

Eventually that money arrived, but by 2003 HPVM still had a $14,000 monthly operating deficit. One morning, representatives from the Ecuadorian Social Security Administration, the IESS, the Instituto Ecuatoriano de Seguridad Social, turned up in Pedro and said, "We hear good things about the hospital and want to see if you'd be interested in providing health care under contract to IESS patients." Unlike the U.S. Social Security system, the IESS builds and operates outpatient clinics and hospitals, many in the same cities where the Ministry of Public Health has built its own set of public hospitals, creating a parallel system. The two remain operationally separate and are staffed by large rival bureaucracies, an inherently awkward and cumbersome arrangement but one that unexpectedly rescued and gave a unique standing to Hospital Pedro Vicente Maldonado. A contract with IESS allowed the hospital to fulfill its mission—and in an Ecuadorian way, with Ecuadorian funds.

It happened at the exact right moment. From the start, the idea was that anyone in and around Pedro with Social Security membership would be eligible for treatment at HPVM, as there were few IESS facilities nearby and no IESS hospitals. In Ecuador, Social Security pays for health care while you're working rather than after you retire. At that time, Social Security covered only 18 percent of the workforce (now it's 45 percent), and though most of the people who were signed up for Social Security had office jobs or were union members, as word got around that HPVM was now a Social Security provider, it substantially boosted the number of people turning up for treatment.

Even better, in 1968 IESS had launched a supplementary *seguro campesino* (rural insurance) program, bringing farmers and fishermen into the system as long as they kept up payments of $2 a month—even less than the policies they weren't buying from Gaus and now wouldn't need, since *seguro campesino* covered an entire family, provided old-age pensions and disability payments, and even helped with funeral costs. "With disbelief and sometimes tears in their eyes," Gaus said, "people said that for the first time they were being taken care of where they lived. Soon they were knocking down our doors."

It wasn't just that people came to the yellow building and were welcomed with smiles; it was that no one was made to feel like a hardship case. From the HPVM point of view, the truly empowering part of an IESS contract—it got signed in 2004—had to do with the surpluses. Well, "surplus" is perhaps a relative term. The point was that IESS had a fixed scale of reimbursements for various procedures—for instance, IESS paid $1,000 for a C-section, which HPVM could perform for $500. Which meant that they would now have enough money to perform another C-section for a truly indigent woman. Or they could "use the margin" and have a $500 lump sum available for other procedures or treatments.

A hospital less focused on how it handled costs might have a smaller surplus or none at all. Gaus had heard stories about IESS contracts with private, for-profit hospitals where the doctors considered any surplus profit, as they were legally entitled to, and maybe bought a boat or built a house; how a surplus got spent was not something IESS concerned itself about. But AHD was and is a nonprofit. "It's exhausting, thinking about costs every minute," Gaus said. "But we don't waste a cent, which keeps us sharp. That's how the community itself lives. Hand to mouth, month to month."

The contract changed the way the hospital conducted business. IESS demanded clinical audits, demonstrating that every medical procedure was documented and that any medications were consistent with a diagnosis, supported by the physical exam and history of each patient. This was the way Adriana came into her own, helping HPVM set up and stay up-to-date with the medical records. Up to that point, AHD's Ecuadorian doctors, who hadn't grown up in what Gaus calls a "culture of documentation," had been far more informal in their record-keeping. Now they also had to compile, separately, an administrative audit for each patient, confirm his or her identity, show a signed authorization for treatment, and make sure the bill submitted matched the services provided. At that point the hospital ran into an even greater challenge, getting the payments they were now properly billing for. The IESS had never dealt with a hospital that took care of as many patients as HPVM did, and the "lag in collectibles" (a technical accounting term Gaus was using again, which means "cash flow problem") could stretch on and on. "Oh, they'll pay," said one IESS veteran, "but maybe not for a year."

This was when Diego Herrera's stall, staving off a creditor for three months, bought critical time. "But," Gaus remembers, "we faced the prospect of closing the hospital if we couldn't figure this one out." The solution was dreamed up by Herrera and put into practice by an old friend from the nonprofit world who dealt with government offices—she outlined the idea in a letter addressed to "Dear Dieguisimo and David." They should get to know each of the people in the IESS payments office personally, she suggested, from the one who received the bills to the one who signed the checks. Many of them, it seemed, felt overworked and underappreciated, if not beleaguered. Reimbursements could get slowed down at a dozen different desks.

Herrera and Gaus also invited the entire IESS team to Pedro for a day that included swimming, volleyball, a soccer game, and lunch. After that, the "service-rendered to payment-received" time dropped to about two months, an interval the hospital could live with and work around. Friendship and gratitude turned out to be far more effective than a bribe, which was how many Ecuadorian businesses approached government offices.

It took a couple of years to hammer out the details. It turned out, for instance, that one IESS director would talk one-on-one only with the "owner of the circus" (an Ecuadorian expression meaning the boss). But by December 2006, HPVM had "crossed the line"—reached the break-even point. The hospital has been self-sufficient ever since and even generates a small profit. In early 2016, IESS renewed its contract with Andean Health and Development, noting that it was particularly pleased that Hospital Pedro Vicente Maldonado used any surplus for indigent care.

Then it was back to Santo Domingo, the noisy, bustling, unexpected city made up of country people from other places, Hólger Velasteguí's *crisol*—crucible—of a new Ecuadorian city. Early each morning in Santo, I had a chance to listen to intensive presentations, mini-lectures, and questions and answers in a smallish rectangular, unadorned, tucked-away conference room in Hospital Hesburgh. Simple green-and-black office chairs surround a central table, which is actually six folding tables pushed together; there's an overhead fluorescent light and a couple of ceiling fans, a floor of white vinyl tiles, and a single piece of high-tech equipment—a video screen for teleconferences with Hospital Pedro Vicente Maldonado, fifty miles away.

Since Santo is practically on the Equator, the sun comes up at pretty much the same time every day, 6:00 or a few minutes after, and the morning meetings, chaired by Diego Herrera and assisted by David Gaus and sometimes Carlos Troya and other doctors, began promptly at 6:30. This made them sunrise sessions—not that you would know it, since the high windows look out only onto interior corridors. The room was crowded with a number of the forty family medicine residents training under contract with the Ministry of Public Health and a few of the six residents in Saludesa's own program.

Looked at one way, these sessions were ordinary enough, part of a tradition established decades ago at teaching hospitals and given its own name: morning report. (The idea of a hospital as an ideal setting for teaching is far more ancient, tracing back to sixth-century Persia.) Though the format varies from one hospital to another, typically the residents, who were on duty overnight, describe newly admitted patients, what they think is wrong with them, and what should be done for them. Staff doctors ask questions and make suggestions. What I hadn't expected was that these sessions would feel like stepping into another crucible.

According to an overview of morning report experiences in the United States and Canada between 1966 and 2011, which appeared in the *Journal of Graduate Medical Education*, these conferences are an "essential component" and the "most visible educational feature" of "residency education throughout different parts of the world." Another article, this one in the *Journal of General Internal Medicine*, says that the potential for learning "is immense—provided that the focus is on education, as opposed to culpability." As David Gaus remembers it, "When I was in med school, a resident had to present at what was called a morbidity and mortality conference, and he or she was humiliated and crucified by the doctor running the meeting."

Another *General Internal Medicine* article suggests that such practices have not altogether disappeared in North America: "Morning report can either be embarrassing, when learners have no idea how to answer a question, or exhilarating, when they do. A well-kept secret amongst faculty members is that they, too, are terrified of morning report. They believe that learners think that they know all the answers and are embarrassed when they miss diagnostic possibilities or have nothing to teach because of limitations in their knowledge."

Nothing like that happens at Hospital Hesburgh, where Gaus and Herrera employ what could be called a "student-side manner" or "doctor-side manner"—a bedside manner for junior colleagues. They treat their residents with respect and as partners in the search for proper treatments. And they all seem to perk up at 7:10 a.m., when several women who work next door in the kitchen bring in trays with toasted cheese sandwiches, juice, pitchers of hot milk and hot water, and a big jar of powdered Nescafé. "If there's one thing residents like to do, it's eat," Gaus said. "So that helps, too. The format is brand-new for them. In med school they probably had morning reports where the attending physician simply said, 'Do this, do that.' No questions, no sense of discovery, no curiosity. Or maybe the resident asked a question and the attending didn't know, so he just deflected it, like a shaman deflecting a magic arrow, and made them look stupid for asking. When he could have said, 'Good question. Let's look it up.'"

"As a teacher," Herrera told me, "you yourself have to have energy and enthusiasm. It's empowering to know stuff that works, apply it, and watch patients, real people lying in beds only a few feet away, get better."

"*We* enjoy learning," Gaus said, and quoted Bob Bitchin, author and sailor, who was born Bob Lipkin, became a traveling companion of Evel Knievel, and then spent thirty-five years cruising the Pacific on yachts: "'The difference between an adventure and an ordeal is attitude.' That's why this unremarkable room is the richest learning place in the hospital."

CHAPTER TWENTY-ONE

A PAIR OF BOOTS

ONCE HOME, I ASKED MIKE HANSEN HOW HE EXPLAINED David Gaus's ability to change and change again. "As a business-man," he said, "I can't. We evaluate risks and rewards, and if something isn't working we cut our losses. But David has a per-sistence and tenacity I've seldom seen. He doesn't just stop doing something if it isn't coming out right—he stays with it and reimagines it until there's a different outcome." Diego does this too, he added.

In Santo I'd made a couple of notes: "Ipsefact" and "Pair of boots." "Ipsefact" referred to Dr. J. Ralph Audy, someone from an earlier generation I'd been reading about and had come to think of as a colleague of Gaus and Herrera, though none had met (Audy died in 1974 at the age of 60). A renowned English tropical medicine researcher who was an M.D. and a Ph.D., Audy was credited with having detected "a plethora of new viruses" in the developing world and was acclaimed for his "inexhaustible supply of jokes, stories, limericks, songs and games"; his "faculty to perceive obscure interrelationships"; and his "wizardry in juggling available funds."

Audy spent half his life in the field—in Africa, India, Burma, and Malaya, beginning with a posting in the early days of World War II as senior medical officer with the Somali Camel Corps—and the last twenty-five years of his life as director of the Hooper Foundation, a research institution in San Francisco. To Audy's way of thinking, all species deliberately modified their environments to improve their chances for health and survival. He called such novel microhabitats—whether they were nests, burrows, cocoons, automobiles, computers, or hospitals—"ipsefacts," meaning artifacts "made by oneself" or, in the case of people, by "skilled workers." He noted that, among people, "Changing societies inherit outmoded but solid urban ipsefacts; and the microhabitats may be unsuited to human efficiency, especially since there is constant feedback between ipsefact and man."

Audy, like Andrija Štampar, saw health—"ample health," he called it, and "the quality of indefeatability"—not so much as a right but as an innate capacity and thought that people strengthened their ability to meet challenges by taking advantage of a succession of human "cocoons," only the first of which, the womb, has been provided by nature.

The next cocoon, he said, is "the mother in the outside world," and as we mature that's followed by the protective support we get from homes, other buildings, family, friends, and the culture we grow up in and its institutions (the "cultural womb"). For Audy, health could be measured "by the degree of protection needed to preserve a steady state."

In "Measurement and Diagnosis of Health," a far-sighted essay Audy wrote in the 1960s, he looked out across the diverse array of ipsefacts and found himself fearing for its unraveling, since "as the population avalanche descends and because of the tempo of change" of modern life, "even the maternal cocoon of the newborn is increasingly unreliable," particularly among underprivileged people. David and Diego were strengthening a spectrum of cocoons in the Ecuadorian countryside, for doctors and patients alike.

"Pair of boots" reminded me of an ancient Central Asian joke passed down by storytellers for centuries. A man walks into a shop full of bits and pieces of all kinds and asks the owner if he has nails, good leather, twine, or dye. In each case the answer is "Yes." This prompts a different question: "Then for heaven's sake why don't you make a pair of boots?"

Gaus and Herrera's decision to make a pair of boots (to become doctors who were teachers) took a lot longer to arrive at than anything that had gone before. The problem was that, Elizabeth Gaus told me, "You can train cleaning people. You can find computer-savvy people, even in a small town. But finding good doctors—that's difficult. Those with specialized training want the top jobs and don't want to work in the countryside. We had to make work in the countryside sexy, irresistible."

Early on HPVM had added a few Quito-trained doctors to the staff, but, as Gaus told me over another dinner at Pescados Dónde Coco (you can never have too many):

Well-trained doctors didn't really exist around Pedro before HPVM, so bringing in Quito doctors was a good step. But the people we hired didn't necessarily understand the needs of the people coming to them. Ecuadorian med students are supposed to get a year of rural medicine, but they're never trained to handle the complexities of these situations, and the only thing they end up learning is that they never want to go to a rural area again. Our doctors would come to Diego and say, "They're not doing what I tell them," and our patients would come to Diego and say, "The docs don't understand what's wrong." It was two *cosmovisiones* not interacting— that of the cosmopolitan Western world and the Andean viewpoint. Yes, all our personnel were Ecuadorian, but there's so much heterogeneity within Ecuador, it was like people speaking two different languages. One of the doctors said, "She wouldn't take the pills for diabetes and blood pressure." But to an Andean mind, if you have to take pills for more than two weeks, it means you're going to a bad doctor. Somehow we had to negotiate our way across this continental divide, to reach an understanding of the chronic conditions modern people have to put up with, diseases that can be tamed but not banished.

In 2007, with HPVM's money problems solved, we finally had a chance to take a breath and think about this. We asked ourselves, "Where do we want to be in ten years?" Frankly, our goal was to transform—and complete—our own hospital, not rural Ecuador. We knew we didn't want to be just building buildings—buildings are only one piece of the puzzle. We wanted a model that worked, something that could be replicated. Along the way we made a big mistake— though fortunately not a very expensive one.

An old friend in La Maná, a town of thirty-two thousand people about four hours south of Pedro, called to say, "I want you to apply your quality care and administrative austerity to our hospital"—a twenty-four-hour Ministry of Public Health [MOH] center that had an operating room. Which was flattering, and seemed, if anything, like a blatant sign from above—since "*la maná*" means manna from heaven or a stroke of luck. We signed an agreement with the town and the ministry, and for six months things went well. We went from zero to thirty surgeries a month, from sixty to a hundred childbirths, and we were only transferring ten patients a month instead of a hundred to Guayaquil, the nearest big city. We introduced laparoscopic surgery—keyhole surgery. We put in some tile and a staircase. We did a lot of cost containment.

But bureaucracy prevented us from stopping the pharmacy from buying huge quantities of useless medicine. Plus we were only there four days a week. Despite all we'd learned in Pedro about cultivating relationships with the community, the hospital director decided to run for mayor—and from a different political party. The worst moment was when a

Ministry of Public Health anesthesiologist, who wasn't an anesthesiologist, gave a woman an overdose; she flatlined, and there was no battery in the defibrillator. We got her back with lidocaine, a drug used for heart attacks. That same day electricity was arcing in the ER. We realized we were in the guts of a Ministry of Public Health hospital—and we pulled out.

If we were going to work with the public sector, we had to own and control the facility. And also this—we tried to hire doctors from Quito, and you know what? We couldn't. It was too far from home, and the chaotic nature of an MOH hospital was too confusing. Plus they didn't understand the culture of a tropical rural area. So we decided to start a residency program at HPVM and reached out to the country's most prestigious university, the Pontifical Catholic University of Ecuador, in Quito—a hospital needs an academic affiliation to become a *hospital docente*, a teaching hospital.

We set up a rigorous program with a fourteen-hour day including three hours of classes, a lot of didactic stuff. It was Ecuador's first rural family medicine program, a three-year program leading to board certification. The Catholic University had its own *urban* family medicine program, dating back to 1987, but by 2012 they'd only produced 266 graduates. Our training marks a real leap into modern medicine, and our residents get really good training in how hospital medicine is supposed to happen. Along the way we learned how to teach them how to approach patients—the *art* of medicine. So we can turn out the five-star doctors the countryside needs.

I'm proud to say that we recently accepted Dr. Katarina Orrico into the program. Dr. Orrico is from Pedro, and an M.D. from Pedro is unusual in itself. Back in 2001, when she was 8, she was Hospital Pedro Vicente Maldonado's very first patient—she was brought in for an allergic reaction. When I saw her again, in her white lab coat at the meeting for new residents, it brought tears to my eyes.

CHAPTER TWENTY-TWO

TELL A REALLY
BIG TRUTH

AHD'S NEW RESIDENCY PROGRAM HAD A PROBLEM: A simple back-of-an-envelope calculation showed that, at the rate HPVM was turning out family physicians (at first, three a year), it would take 492 years to populate rural Ecuador with the five-star doctors it needed. It was this realization that prompted AHD to own, build, and staff a second, bigger hospital—Hospital Hesburgh. That and a study by the University of California at Berkeley's business school, funded by AHD, that showed that Santo Domingo and its surrounding area's 600,000 people had "a very large unmet health care need," and a new hospital could "greatly expand the family physician training program" and would also give AHD "potential national visibility"—since the catchment area of patients was nearly nine times larger than the 70,000 people who can get to Hospital Pedro Vicente Maldonado.

Another part of the motivation to build another hospital was the feeling "If we discover something, why keep it under a stone?" Gaus said that "as a town, Pedro Vicente Maldonado, which means so much to us, is Nowheresville—to Ecuadorians." And there was a push from Fr. Hesburgh, then 92. As Gaus told me on a drive between Pedro and Santo:

> My relationship with him evolved from profound respect to profound fondness. He got more protective of me and gave me more personal advice. In the beginning, I had to call his secretary and schedule appointments, but later it was "Just put him on." Fr. Ted got more confident about what we could do, but he was always one step ahead, though he left the specifics up to us. When HPVM got to 40 percent sustainability, he said, "When will you get to 50?" And at 50, "When will you reach 100?"
>
> Often he said, "If you're going to tell the truth, tell a really big truth. That'll capture people's imaginations." This time he said, "It's time to go to scale. A project like this could give you continent-wide visibility, but you guys will have to pull it off. Every great movement needs a prototype, something that can work that's not a bunch of *norteamericanos* doing all the heavy lifting. Ecuador is a key country. If you do it there, it can be done next door in Peru and Bolivia, maybe all over Latin America. A step in a long journey."

Diego Herrera did the heaviest lifting. A study by grad students at the Haas Business School at U-Cal Berkeley confirmed what Gaus and Herrera had already recognized—that Santo Domingo was in urgent need of higher-quality health care services. Herrera had already scouted the old four-acre Santo high school as a possible site, and then, based on what he had learned at HPVM, he figured out that over $5 million could be saved simply by working with local builders he and Gaus knew to be reliable; as a result, the final cost was half of the $10 million price tag

Quito contractors had been quoting. Without cutting corners: Hospital Hesburgh is a fifty-thousand-square-foot facility with full critical care, ER, and outpatient services—and that striking landscaping.

But some *norteamericano* assistance was still needed. A couple of foundations with Notre Dame ties found the project compelling: Ronald McDonald House Charities, which has extensive overseas contacts, and—maybe more surprisingly—the Harry and Jeanette Weinberg Foundation, which mostly funds projects in Maryland, Hawaii, and Israel. Weinberg, whose parents emigrated from Eastern Europe to Baltimore when he was 3, left school after sixth grade and eventually became the largest single real estate investor in Hawaii. At his death in 1990, he left $1 billion to his foundation "to provide direct services to low-income and vulnerable populations," saying of other foundations, "While they are finding cures for all the ills of the world, someone will be hungry, someone will be cold. That's our job."

Midsized donations came from lots of people in Gaus's Class of '84 (the "friends of Dave," they called themselves), and the most innovative fundraising came from a Class of '70 Domer, John C. Rudolf, a Seattle investment adviser, AHD board member, mountain climber (having conquered seven of the eight tallest peaks in the world), and long-distance bike rider. He enlisted a bunch of his own super-fit and high-achieving friends, notably Dave Cutler, a software engineer who invented the Windows operating systems—meaning, says an admirer, that he "influences the computing experiences of two billion people."

The group arranged a series of weeklong charity bike rides that, in its first five years, raised $1 million. A more recent tour by eighteen cyclists covered the four hundred miles between Glacier National Park in Montana and Jasper National Park in Alberta, Canada; it involved twenty-four thousand feet of uphill pedaling along mountain roads—the equivalent, a celebratory video noted, "of three to four Tour de France stages spread over seven days."

These strategies have been of particular value lately, since it may take Hospital Hesburgh longer to achieve full sustainability than it did HPVM. It's easier now for AHD to sell insurance policies to companies, since that market is gaining traction, but IESS, having built its own hospital in Santo Domingo, is only reimbursing Hospital Hesburgh for high-ticket services such as the use of the Intensive Care Unit or the MRI (magnetic resonance imaging) machine that IESS doesn't offer in its Santo facility. And IESS has been in a budget squeeze since 2015, when the international price of the oil that Ecuador exports (and depends on for the Correa administration's social programs) dropped from $155 a barrel to $28 a barrel before recovering to $45 a barrel. IESS also faced having to rebuild two Pacific Coast hospitals that were severely damaged in the April 2016 earthquake that killed 673 people and injured 28,000.

One afternoon over a cup of coffee in the Hospital Hesburgh *cafetería*, Diego Herrera told me the story of how AHD itself became part of Correa's reforms when, in 2011, a former classmate of Herrera's became an assistant secretary of health, got President Correa's ear, and told Correa all about the advantages of specialized training for family physicians and how a successful model had already been set up at a small rural hospital halfway between Quito and the coast. Herrera said:

> Correa had already decided to give every kid in the country a shot at a university education. If they could pass a standardized test and show language proficiency, they could even get a full scholarship to Oxford or Harvard or Stanford. The payback would be several years of work at a mid-level government job. Now Correa wanted a total overhaul of physician training. Up to that point, the office of the president had tamed or reformed every ministry—except the Ministry of Public Health, where the average tenure of a Minister of Public Health was six months. This made it hard to create any long-term plan or vision. But Correa had just appointed as

minister Carina Vance Mafla, a woman born in the United States and with a U. S. degree in public health. She made a stir as the first openly gay cabinet member and shut down "gay cure" clinics in the country. She was excited about a residency program.

Less than a quarter of Ecuador's twenty thousand doctors have residency training—the rest are GPs, general practitioners, some of them knowledgeable, some not so much, and no real way to find out which is which. Traditionally there's been a lot of "no man's land" in Ecuadorian medicine—you get your degree and then go off to do as you please. The government's goal is to create twenty thousand board-certified specialists of one sort or another—internists, surgeons, the full array. An enormous project. But their more immediate goal is to train a thousand family physicians as the "workhorses of the new residency model"—the minister's phrase. This represents a profound cultural shift, one that essentially means starting from scratch, like in the first family medicine programs back in the U. S. in the 1950s. In the 1980s Ecuador imported English M. D.s to train the first local family physicians, but this time David and I, in our little hospital in Pedro, started getting calls and found ourselves joining a ministry-funded, eight-university consortium set up to develop a three-year curriculum that would in effect mass-produce family physicians. In this case the payback will be that once they graduate, the residents will work for a rural ministry hospital for six years. One of our board members said, "AHD went from being the story of David's midlife crisis to being about Ecuador's midlife crisis."

It was a long, arduous process, but everything we've done up to now leads to this. We thought that by having a second hospital, we could take the resident program from six doctors to fifteen. Instead it's exploded: In January 2014, six months *before* Hospital Hesburgh was ready to take in patients, we were working with dozens of Ministry of Public

Health residents, using five of our graduates as teachers. We held classes in our unfinished building and then took everyone—teachers and students alike—to the ministry hospital in Santo for direct, hands-on experience. There were sixty residents at first, which was a stretch even for us, so we pared it down to forty-five. A quantum leap, even so. Sometimes I'm still pinching myself. Has this really happened?

"DDx" is medical shorthand for "differential diagnosis," a mainstay of morning report at Hospital Hesburgh, as the two residents coming off night duty present their findings. No one knows why so many medical abbreviations end in a small "x," but probably they derive from the widely familiar "Rx" for "prescription," which itself is most likely a rendering of the Latin imperative word *recipe*, meaning "Take this!" Other common medical abbreviations include "Sx," "Hx" and "FHx," which stand for "symptom," "medical history," and "family history," all of which lead up to a "Dx," a "medical diagnosis," and the proper "Tx," or "treatment."

A differential diagnosis is of particular importance because, when it comes to things likely to go wrong and land you in the hospital, there are fewer symptoms than there are potential problems. "A range of causes of conditions," one textbook says, using more technical terms, "can show similar presenting symptoms." Fever, for instance—what's the likelihood it's caused by one thing or another? A differential diagnosis is arrived at by assembling all the possibles and, after research, examining and questioning a patient, "building a case" by systematically eliminating the improbables—a process called "R/O" for "ruling out"—and drawing conclusions that, when you're a resident, will be presented, commented on, questioned, and perhaps challenged at morning report.

At any teaching hospital, a residency is a somewhat abrupt transition from the theoretical to the practical, and morning report is when feedback is most immediate because real patients are either getting better or not. The conversations I observed at these meetings felt unusually intense in their quiet way—controlled lightning bolts.

Quiteño doctors' not understanding the rural *cosmovisión* was a subject that kept coming up. One morning Diego said, "Let's say you come up with a treatment plan that will cost $30 and the patient only has $8. Unless you address the problem up front, the treatment's a nonstarter. So you might say, 'Often people get anxious about one of three things—the diagnosis, the medicine, or the payment. Could it be that one of these things is giving you anxiety?'"

And *un*learning seemed to take up as much time as learning. "There's so much the *quiteños* haven't been exposed to, even in Quito," a visiting U. S. med student told me after one morning report. "They've been socialized *not* to ask questions. Their energy gets suppressed." Herrera and Gaus brought this up at a debriefing an hour later, over more coffee in the *cafetería*. "Until ten years ago," Herrera said, "college graduates in Ecuador never had to write a paper that would teach them how to organize their thoughts with a thesis statement and supporting details. Or read a book and take meaning from it. It's a poor country—there aren't that many books. They're a luxury. People Xerox chapters."

"One of the first questions Diego asks residents," Gaus said, "is, 'What's the last book you read?' Nine out of ten put their head down. So they learn how to hide their ignorance. Almost the entire educational strategy they've been exposed to is fatally flawed. So we tell them, 'What you know about learning—throw it out the window.'"

"We push hard," Herrera agreed. "Clear thought processes are the prerequisites for building a case. Get the emphasis right, and find the right details. Sometimes a resident will say something like, 'Mr. Cruz, who is 60, came in with shortness of breath. He lives in Golondrinas, three hours away. He's been fighting with his daughter, and she says her mom says he's been drinking too much, and she bought him a green shirt for his birthday.'"

"It's not that they're gossips," Gaus said. "They're observant; they're bright; they're good storytellers. They're M.D.s. But they've never even looked stuff up on the Internet—basically they had to move overnight from rote learning and getting their information orally to the Internet. So many bad habits. Medical ones, too. It used to be thought that if you push on someone's belly you could feel the tubes connecting the kidneys to the bladder. Rubbish! Or that you could hear amoebas in the belly through a stethoscope. We have to break the cycle—and it's very much a cycle. The med schools would say, 'They came to us that way.' Colleges say the same thing. And the high schools and the grade schools. It's an astonishing country, but historically it never put much emphasis on education. So many parents never put a pencil in a kid's hand or showed them colors or recited the days of the week or the months of the year. It's not insurmountable, but if you don't peel off those layers, you won't be effective. We get it— it's not anyone's fault. What makes us unique here is we've taken this on and stay focused on it."

"We do have some attrition in the program," Herrera said. "Particularly at the start. Some miss mom's rice in Quito, or a girlfriend or a husband, or they say the program is too tough. We're not here to be cuddly, warm and fuzzy. We're not about mediocrity—mediocrity doesn't transform a country. We push back on anyone who says, 'Dilute it a little.' Or 'It's good enough for Ecuador.' This is too important. Otherwise we fail the population and the doctors themselves."

"What we can do," Gaus said, "is turn them into perceivers rather than receivers. What works, what eventually kicks in, even if it takes the entire first year, is that they're always in the company of mentors, our own graduates. We stay beside them as they work, live it with them, read any Internet articles we assign. What aspect of training will stay with them forever? The patients? The facility? No—the mentoring, the challenging, the injection of passion, curiosity, and enthusiasm, the constant commitment to learning, the fact that we, too, are always learning more. We see them get hungry to look beyond each particular case. Afterwards, those who make it say, 'That was the most intensive experience of my life.'"

This produces an almost chemical change in the systems of young doctors serving rural Ecuador—they want to do more. It felt like a real-life working out of Fr. Ted's favorite prayer—"Lord, give bread to those who are hungry, and to those who have bread, give them a hunger for justice."

CHAPTER TWENTY-THREE

HEALTH IN ECUADOR—THE NEXT TEN YEARS

AROUND THE WORLD, ACCORDING TO A WIDELY READ 2010 overview report, "2,420 medical schools, 467 schools or departments of health, and an indeterminate number of postsecondary nursing educational institutions train about 1 million new doctors, nurses, midwives, and public health professionals every year."

This study is the Frenk Report—so called to honor its lead writer, Dr. Julio Frenk, a former secretary of health in Mexico and dean of the Harvard School of Public Heath, and currently president of the University of Miami. By design it appeared exactly a hundred years after the Flexner Report, a landmark look at U.S.

and Canadian med schools so influential it upended the entire medical profession and was hailed as "the most important event in the history of American and Canadian medical education."

Abraham Flexner, an education reformer, later founded the Institute for Advanced Study at Princeton, Albert Einstein's academic home for the last two decades of his life. Many old-time medical schools, one modern description of them says, were "loose and lax" and "lacked defined standards or goals beyond the generation of financial gain." Thanks to Flexner's sweeping recommendations, med schools got a scientific underpinning anchored by the germ theory of disease, then a recent discovery; it's one reason so many doctors wear the white coats found in science labs. Med schools also became part of universities, with a rigorous curriculum in which two years of lectures were followed by two years of hands-on training, the origin of "See one, do one, teach one."

Flexner's North American reforms, quickly copied in Europe, "contributed to the doubling of life span during the 20th century," the Frenk Report points out. Fifty years later, a "second generation" of reforms introduced "problem-based learning" (PBL), giving med students real problems to reason through and solve. Dr. Howard Barrows, the PBL founder, discovered that if it stayed theoretical, the basic neuroscience information he was teaching his first-year students at McMaster University Medical School in Hamilton, Ontario, vanished from their memories as rapidly as random "nonsense syllables." A year later, as sophomores, they could no longer pass their first-year tests.

For all its brilliance, Flexner's work had serious shortcomings: Although his Princeton institute became a home for Einstein at a time when Ivy League colleges still had a "Jewish quota," Flexner himself viewed African Americans as inferior, and for the next fifty years many U. S. medical schools had no black students. There were also few openings for women.

Julio Frenk's main concern is with a growing imbalance: "A large proportion of the 7 billion people who inhabit our planet are trapped in the health conditions of a century earlier." As a result, "a slow-burning crisis is emerging," marked by a "mismatch of professional competencies to patient and population priorities." He praises the post–Alma Ata work of primary health care workers, like the *behvarzan* in Iran or Pakistan's Lady Health Workers, who receive six months of training to work with three-quarters of the rural population in their homes. But looking beyond that, what's immediately needed is a third generation of reforms, grounded in yet another new approach: "Only postsecondary education can endow professionals to perform complex reasoning, deal with uncertainty, anticipate and plan impending changes." So in the twenty-first century "almost all the most successful leaders of the health sector are professionals with postsecondary education."

The Frenk Report sounds a lot as if it's describing AHD's family resident training program. When I mentioned this to Gaus, he said there was no direct connection because he hadn't met Frenk when the report came out, and back in 2010 the team of Herrera and Gaus had yet to graduate their first few residents. So maybe it was a case of convergent thinking under the pressure of urgency. Gaus, who got a chance to meet Frenk only several years later, made a point of telling him that AHD thinks of itself as dedicated to doing what Frenk had said needs doing. "Absolutely, yes, you are. Congratulations," Frenk said. "So far there hasn't been much progress, or at least not enough progress, in other places."

However, the Frenk Report itself predicts slow going. Gaus pointed me to this passage: "One of the main challenges of the health professions is their urban bias and thus the reluctance of many of their members to work in remote rural areas among underprivileged populations."

As Gaus said during a recent conversation:

It's early days yet, even if 2017 marks our twentieth anniversary. We have to go on doing what we're doing, growing the ranks of family physicians mentored by people who've lived the rural piece of doctoring. Yeah, we have cool stuff to train on, like Rosa the SimMom, who can talk, wink, and breathe, and sure, once they're certified specialists, family physicians can earn higher salaries, maybe $2,500 a month instead of $1,000. But it's the mentoring, as in any field—medicine, public health, sports, and business—that's such a strong predictor of someone's future. Look at the twelve apostles—they had a pretty good mentor, and they were all rural people! So far we've graduated twenty of our own residents, and fourteen are in the rural realm, committed to those populations, teaching or practicing at Ministry of Public Health facilities or here with us at our hospitals. One of our graduates works exclusively in the countryside two hours north of Quito, and one is a residency director down in Loja, an eleven-hour drive to the south.

As the Frenk Report recognizes, health in the countryside has to have curative *and* preventive services, on a permanent basis. So we'll keep putting highly qualified doctors out there—doctors who get it, who have a feel for the place, who can think on their feet, and once they graduate we have to foster and nurture them, and cheer them on. There are no alumni associations here in Latin America, but we'll stay in touch with former residents now at rural MOH clinics. The former residents working here will text and Skype with them about the challenges still faced by pregnant women in small villages. This kind of "telemedicine lite"—low-cost, lowish-tech, and doctor-to-doctor—plus an ambulance we plan to buy can help our alumni do something to shorten what are called "the three delays" that lead to many maternal deaths: delay in seeking care, delay in getting to a health facility, delay in getting adequate care.

This is something we hope to see in the next ten years. It's how our model works. Expose people to opportunities and great things. And hope.

I asked Gaus if he was talking about Ecuadorian hope. He said:

More like a cohort of hope. Something new on our horizon, the Andean Health Institute [AHI], can broaden this fellowship—taking on things like the updating of our medical manual, which, since it's been on the Internet, has been consulted by doctors around Latin America. Also putting out more issues of *Práctica Familiar Rural* [Rural Family Practice], a quarterly journal unique in Ecuador, which we launched in 2015. With U.S. universities as our partners, AHI can set up and coordinate research projects that'll define the questions the developing world needs to ask. Like looking beyond Zika to the next viral infections.

How does antibiotic resistance affect Ecuadorians? In relation to stomach ulcers, for instance. For decades the assumption was that stress caused ulcers—or spicy food, or liquor, or just dumb, bad luck. Until an Australian scientist showed, and won a Nobel Prize for it, that it's an infection caused by bacteria in the digestive tract. No matter where you live, a fifth of the people with these bacteria will get ulcers. But—a big but—maybe only a third of North Americans are harboring these bacteria, while in Ecuador it's 90 percent of the population. The two most common antibiotics for treating ulcers have been overprescribed in this country for decades, for colds and aches and pains, with the result, of course, that the bacteria are resistant to both drugs. We're looking into treatments that can help Ecuadorians. As an aside, how did these bugs reach so many Ecuadorian stomachs? A new study links their presence to the "Columbian Exchange," suggesting that European and African stomach bacteria displaced those harbored by American Indian populations and then somehow became more virulent. But until this information can be connected to cures for stomach ulcers, it'll just be the latest nugget in a shiny pile of ten thousand interesting things.

Hey, we're a nonprofit. It's not our job to reach everything and everyone—we can't replace the state. We're not big enough. We don't have and we don't want the political power to run things. We work indirectly—as Fr. Ted did. We accompany and catalyze. We've got a program that doesn't exist anywhere else yet. We're training tomorrow's five-star doctors. This doesn't make us heroes. I don't feel like a hero. But in Ecuador I feel like I've got my hand on the pulse of humanity.

Afterword

Hospital Hesburgh achieved financial self-sustainability in 2018. It finally happened, but required the same boost Hospital Pedro Vicente Maldonado needed: the public sector. It affirmed much of what we had worked on for twenty years—and in a way that let us see what can happen over the next twenty years. In most instances, there simply is not enough economic support in rural areas of lower-income countries for communities to pay out of pocket exclusively. That model would provide care for the "haves" of the community but likely leave the "have-nots" without coverage. Some degree of public-sector support is vital.

Very early on we realized—well, after we were told this by our patients!—that to be of any use to a rural community a health facility has to heal those who are already sick, not just prevent healthy people from getting sick (then the prevailing assumption around the world). Otherwise why bother seeing a doctor at all?

We had to build hospitals, not just outpatient clinics. But then we ran up against another prevailing assumption: that a private rural hospital could never pay for itself and would forever have to depend on the generosity of (in most cases) *norteamericanos* who lived thousands of miles away. After trying a lot of ideas that didn't work, or didn't work well enough, we established workable—and unprecedented—partnerships with the public sector. In Pedro Vicente Maldonado, Ecuador's Social Security system is the critical public partner. At Hospital Hesburgh in Santo Domingo, it was the Ministry of Public Health.

Of course we'll probably still find ourselves in a state of cash-flow emergency into the foreseeable future, but hospitals function the way communities live. The public-sector reimbursements, though generous, often take six months or a year to make their way through the bureaucracy. But they *do* come through. The model works.

So where do we go from here? Since the model works, can it be exported or taken to scale? Believe me, we think about this question every day. We have a system of hospitals and clinics that offer services to a large population. We have a physician-training program that continues to graduate Ecuadorian family physicians. Expanding that network to a broader population throughout the Ecuadorian countryside—or into other Andean countries—is a strong possibility. But Diego Herrera and our U.S. board have pushed us to think beyond the network, even beyond its extension, and share what we've learned about how things work out in the countryside, lessons rarely found in scientific or academic literature.

We've already taken steps. Our online Saludesa medical manual, introduced in 2010, focuses on the best practices for rural Latin America. The first two editions stayed within the traditional biomedical paradigm—disease-based, biologically driven—but conveyed information in a way that took into account the rural context, where specialists and equipment routinely available in cities are often absent. In the third edition we broadened our focus to include the cultural aspects of diseases, the Andean viewpoint that Ecuadorian physicians need to be thoroughly familiar with to understand rural communities well enough to negotiate and humanize the patient-doctor encounter. It's where *The Washington Manual of Medical Therapeutics* finally meets the anthropologist and the sociologist.

In 2016 we decided to publish our own online scientific journal in order to share research findings that are uniquely Ecuadorian and likely to be overlooked by European or U.S.-based journals. Our budget for research is small but is boosted and strengthened by our collaboration with the University of Notre Dame's Eck Institute for Global Health and the University of Wisconsin's Global Health Institute. Undertaking the journal has been a monumental and critical step for a country where very few physicians and public-health specialists have engaged in research—even at the university level.

To our delight and surprise, these two online, Spanish-language publications receive more than eight thousand visits a month from at least half a dozen countries. It's clear from this response that global public health requires new and creative indicators to measure the impacts that health care systems have on the communities they serve. This is particularly true now that the small rural or district hospital is finally finding its way into the primary health care literature as an essential component of health-service delivery in low- to middle-income countries.

I DRIVE THE ROAD FROM QUITO TO THE COUNTRYSIDE every week. It's wildly beautiful; lush vegetation covers the steep mountains, brilliant sunrises and sunsets flood the skies. But that twisting, pot-holed highway that clings so desperately to the side of the western slopes of the Andes, with the mudslides, small floods, and occasional downed power lines that threaten it, perfectly reflects the danger lurking within the beauty. My thoughts frequently return to Alfredo, the seven-year-old boy bitten by a pit viper who came to me less than a year after I started working in Pedro Vicente Maldonado, years before we built our hospital there. I still hear his voice—*"Doc, voy a morir"*—"Doc, I'm going to die." That road was his lifeline, his lone chance for survival—if he could make it to the capital for snake anti-venom in time.

He didn't. The road let him down. The health care system let him down. We let him down.

The road represents the hope of connecting rural with urban, pre-modern with modern, the forgotten with the privileged few. It also symbolizes the complexity of human health and health care delivery. The road, in fact, is but one necessary component of a highly complex mosaic.

Health problems are staggeringly complex on the global level. Commitments and sophisticated approaches incorporating the biological sciences, the social sciences, public health, economics, and politics—that's where we are more likely to find the answers. The road stretches ahead.

David Gaus

Index

TONY HISS, an author, lecturer, and consultant on restoring America's cities and landscapes, is the author of thirteen books, including *The Experience of Place*, *The View from Alger's Window*, and *In Motion: The Experience of Travel*. Hiss was a staff writer at the New Yorker for more than thirty years, and since then has been a visiting scholar at New York University.